RUSSIA

THE ESSENTIAL GUIDE FOR THE BUSINESS TRAVELLER

JOHN MATTOCK

SUPPORTED BY SMIRNOFF VODKA

First published in 1996

Kogan Page Limited
120 Pentonville Road
London N1 9JN

British Library Cataloguing in Publication Data

A CIP record for this book is available from the British Library.

ISBN 0 7494 1964 4

Typeset by Transet Ltd., Coventry, England.
Printed in England by Clays Ltd, St Ives plc

In memory of my father, John Mattock — a bricklayer who loved Ivan Denisovich

Statistics are estimates and information is presented as a matter of opinion. While the editors strive for accuracy and detail, this document should not be considered strictly factual. It is a general introduction to culture, an initial step in building bridges of understanding between peoples. It may not apply to all peoples of the nation. You should therefore consult other sources for more information.

Culturgram '95: Russia (Russian Federation),
Brigham Young University

As a Russia-preneur, you are an apostle of free enterprise, for good or ill. Your business should be a beacon of hope, your profit margins a paean of liberty. Let your activities bring employment to the Russian people. Let your conduct bring honor to America.

Richard Poe, *How to Profit from the Coming Russian Boom*

There's no point in expecting someone who's warm to understand someone who's cold.

Alexander Solzhenitsyn, *One Day in the Life of Ivan Denisovich*

Listen now, lads,
To what your grandad says.
Our land might be rich,
But it's a right old mess.

Alexey Konstantinovich Tolstoy, poet & playwright (1817–75)
(Author's translation)

Contents

How this book is constructed

We have imagined a Westerner going on a business trip to Russia, where he meets a Russian counterpart, Yevgenii, and gets to know him.

We follow the process from preparation, through the journey, into the business dealings and closer to Yevgenii himself.

For each step of the way, we offer material and ideas to make the experience fruitful in terms of learning. Any novice who really undertakes such a journey and follows these patterns of thinking will become wiser about the Russians, and do better business in Russia as a result.

HOW TO USE THIS BOOK

- Read it from front to back at a sitting, then shove it in your briefcase the next time you go to Russia. Then scribble notes all over it.

or

- Skim it, until you find an idea or topic that appeals to you. Read more deeply about this issue elsewhere, and steer your conversations with Russians into this area. Then you build your model from a starting point of your own choosing.

or

- Just dip into it at random and find a bit to show your neighbour on the plane to Sheremetevo.

THE BILINGUAL FORMAT

For Westerners who cannot read the Cyrillic alphabet, the first short phrase list (on page 63) is transliterated back into the Roman alphabet using a simple system.

The 'Business Phrasebook' later on is pitched at 'low intermediate' level. If you are a Russian with 'Gymnasium English', or a Westerner with 'evening-class Russian', then this section will help you to do business in that foreign language.

After the section on 'The Language', all Russian words appear in the Latin alphabet. The stress-mark tells you which syllable to emphasise.

Obviously we could not include for our Russian readers full and separate briefings on the USA, France, Japan and the rest. Instead, we offer a behavioural guide for the international working culture — 'The Western Way', in Russian at the end of the book. It aims to help the Russian understand how a Westerner might communicate at meetings, in presentations, during negotiations.

Цель данной книги заключается в том, чтобы помочь западным бизнесменам лучше узнать привычки, традиции и поведение русских, понять их взгляды на жизнь, мотивы и отношение к бизнесу. Книга также включает в себя два раздела, предназначенные помочь русским бизнесменам в общении с иностранцами – деловой разговорник (русско-англнйский), и зссе на русском о том как бизнесмены с Запада ведут переговоры, делают презентации и т.д.. Наша цель поддержать деловые начинания и всячески способствовать здоровому бизнесу. Желаем Вам удачи!

Introduction

Please feel free to skip this introductory essay. You can dip into this book wherever you like.

SCHIZOPHRENICS AND SLEAZE BAGS

This is a practical and positive book about Russia. It aims to help you make sense of your visit there, if you expect to be doing any kind of work or business with Russians.

The lists of Western publishers are clogged with sardonic-pessimistic-sensationalist exposés of criminality, double-dealing, and the unreliability of the post-Soviet business world — not to mention the post-Bolshevik Russian personality.

It is gloomy stuff, and people are fed up with it.

> “*...the richest crop of books on a given subject is harvested just as readers' interest is at its nadir... the subject [is] out of the headlines. Market conditions for books about Russia are said to be tough.*”
>
> Mary Dejevsky, *The Independent*, 31/12/94

That said, we have tried to avoid the use of rose-tinted spectacles. We suggest in this book many attitudes and habits which are hangovers from the days of *homo sovieticus*. If you are dealing with a Russian over the age of 30, he will have ways of seeing things and ways of acting that might confuse you or make you uncomfortable. His perceptions seldom conform to the case studies at Harvard Business School.

In the Brezhnev era, the business-traveller stories brought back from Moscow, Leningrad or Kiev concerned the intricacies of counter-trade deals: *They wanted to pay me in tractor tyres and beetroot...*or the pressures of local hospitality: *Seven kinds of vodka, and then I was stupid enough to mention that I'd been a speed-skater in my student days. We were out on the frozen river at 2 am*....or local negotiating style: *They knew my visa expired the next day, but they kept delaying the price discussion; then they hit me with a demand for a 20% cut in the car on the way to the airport*...or the bizarre symptoms of the centrally planned economy and the Five Year Plan: *He actually asked me to* understate *the performance of the machine I was selling, so he could safely push it beyond those limits and look good to his bosses*...or the latest whispered joke: *What's a kilometre long and lives on potatoes? A meat queue in Tomsk.*

The gags these days retain the same long-suffering quality — and a lot of self deprecation.

> “*Will Russia ever have a fully functioning market economy?*
>
> *Why not? We already have a* malfunctioning *market economy...*”
>
> Boris Fedorov, former Finance Minister

(This quip goes back at least as far Count Sergei Yulevich Witte, finance minister in the 1890s — another time when Russia was desperately trying to attract foreign investment: ‘The world should be surprised that we have *any* government in Russia, not that we have an imperfect government.’)

How does business work in Russia today?

> “*Two people meet. The first one says: ‘You want to buy a cartload of sugar?’ The second one replies: ‘Yes, fine.’ They agree on price. Then the first one goes to see if he can buy a cartload of sugar, and the second goes to see if he can find some money.*”
>
> Joke doing the rounds

Much of the recent literature has naturally focused on business activities and opportunities — *Adam Smith Goes to Moscow, How to Profit from the Coming Russian Boom, Capitalising on the New Russia* — and scattered through these books and articles are tips on dealing with *The Russian Character.*

The same themes recur time and again, and the commentary sometimes sinks pretty low:

"Russia is mentally ill; it is schizophrenic."

Vadim Viazmin, self-taught psychoanalyst

This is a wrong attitude. If we designate a whole society as sick, what are we saying about the individuals who make up that society? And where does that leave us when we try do work with them?

It *isn't* all mad, and you *can* do business there — and build good relationships that bring results. This book helps you take the first steps, or review the progress you have made so far.

The usual topical tips and handy hints are here, and the context is not idealised. Any enterprise in Russia from now until the millennium will take place against the background of a society and economy in turmoil, with all the well recorded ugliness and injustice of a system in transition. We have not dwelt on the ugliness, but we hope we have been realistic.

The poisons that built up during generations of totalitarianism are spilling out now, and extremes of misbehaviour are common — criminality, corruption, broken promises. As resources have been transformed into hard currency, and the *valuta* has fled the country, it has been the selfish, the unscrupulous and the well connected who have made the headlines.

The Western* business partners who have assisted in the process have not all been paragons of ethical behaviour, either:

"It's like the old Texas oil-boom towns, a constant parade of con-men, promoters and shady customers...the greatest collection of sleaze bags in the world."

Robert Strauss, US Ambassador

---

* *Western/ Westerner* will be used to denote the visitor to Russia — the business person to whom most of this book is addressed — and the non-communist/ 'free' world outside the Soviet Empire. For these purposes, developed economies in the East are 'western'. (The trade in Japanese used cars is highly developed around Vladivostok; the fisheries of Siberia do business with South Korea.)

Please note: it was the *American* business people Ambassador Strauss was describing. The proceeds from this grubby, grabbing business environment have become capital to feed growth elsewhere in the economy. (As the proceeds from mob activities still do in America; as did proceeds from the opium and slave trades in England. Why not the same process in Russia?)

Certain observers find cause for optimism in this dank corner of the world's business affairs:

> *"In the short term hope lies in the business class, the former Communists, the criminal and the less criminal, wanting to turn respectable. Theirs are the victors' spoils, part of which could be ploughed back into the country from their Swiss bank accounts."*
>
> John Kampfner, *Inside Yeltsin's Russia*

Russian diplomatic and commercial staff who come and talk to business seminars in the West often face hostile questions about crime and corruption. They have developed a sobering response: *Of course it exists; there is no point in denying it. I have no answers except to say that we have an awful lot of work to do.*

Over a drink later, the same spokesmen for The New Russia will sometimes corroborate Ambassador Strauss's observation, and find a strain of hypocrisy in some of the prurient outrage in the Western media. If the West was expecting a class of upstanding business experts to emerge, full of mature integrity, then the first wave of Western business people to come in at *perestroika* time set a poor example.

If a Russian was selling a $15000 sable coat for $1000 cash, or arranging shipments of minerals or caviar that had evaporated from state inventories, or circumventing export controls on antiques and works of art, then a Westerner — individual or corporate — was buying the goods.

With such contracts we do not concern ourselves; it is difficult to give advice on 'How to Build Good Business Relationships While Checking Over Your Shoulder for the Police'.

The right approach to another culture is to set about *building a model.* You keep it flexible, and feed fresh information into it so it can grow and become more complex — just like the reality.

Prejudices are generally held to be damaging; stereotypes make us insensitive and inflexible; mental sets exist in all of us and we should examine our own with care

The ideas and information here* should give you a starting point for building your model. If you already know Russia a little, you might find fresh building material here. But we cannot help you to model the Russian criminal — schizophrenic or otherwise; and Western sleaze bags will probably not enjoy this book.

---

* Some of the *ideas* are developed at length, in essays and imaginary dialogues. These concern Russian attitudes and behaviour that might directly affect their business dealings with foreigners.

Much of the information is in very abbreviated form, and intended only to give a hint, insight or appetising tit-bit. To learn more about 'Minister Zhdanov and his cronies' [page 114], or the nineteenth century literary theme of 'the superfluous man' [page 149], you will need to consult encyclopedias and textbooks, or your new Russian friends).

BUILDING A MODEL OF A CULTURE

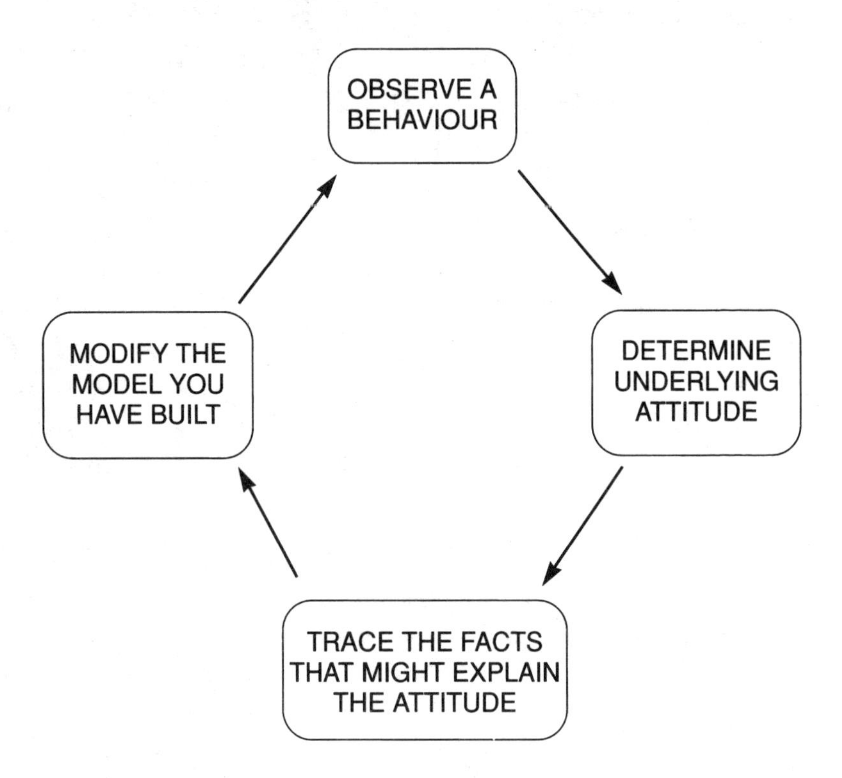

- ***Facts:*** Population density; economic history; family/tribal structure; religion; topography; climate; laws; news and information media...
- ***Attitudes*** (and values)*:* Business before pleasure? Or vice-versa?; Naturally rebellious? Or happy subordinates?; Spiritual or materialistic?; Ingenuous or secretive?; Cosmopolitan or parochial?...
- ***Behaviour:*** Do they stick to the agenda? Make jokes about the boss? Invite you home for dinner? Insist on having everything in writing? Welcome challenges — or hide from them? Keep promises — or let you down?...

This process is subjective; the model you build will be *your* model. There are links between background facts, the values of the people, and the way those values make them behave. Although you will never prove those links scientifically, your model will hold everything together. Without it all your observations will remain a random and unconnected jumble.

The whole exercise must be driven by curiosity. In 1980, a curious traveller was motoring across White Russia (Belarus).

> *"Already the country...was slow, impersonal and absolute. I could not help wondering what effect such isolation might have on its inhabitants...Was the easy Russian submission to God or tyranny, I wondered, the result of a people crushed by the sheer size of their land? Could it be that the meandering, mystical, rough-hewn qualities of the Russian psyche — Russian novels, Russian music — that the unwieldy immensity of Russian bureaucracy...*
>
> *But this froth of irresponsible questions subsided unanswered at a sign which said 'Minsk Campsite'..."*
>
> Colin Thubron, *Among the Russians*

PUSHKIN'S YEVGENII

The 'easy Russian submission to ... tyranny' dates from a long time before Stalin.

Three hundred years ago it was already a delicate and dangerous subject, discussed *in secret* by conspirators of various persuasions. (The image of the Russian agitator with snow on his boots and a bomb in his pocket goes back to the mid-nineteenth century; the paranoid behaviour of the Tsars goes back to Ivan the Terrible.)

The only *public* forum was literature, where issues like abuse of power, social injustice and the corrupt 'system' were probed in more or less oblique ways. Short stories, poems and, as the 19th century advanced, great novels and plays were produced, which can be read in sequence as a socio-politico-ideological history of the century — if you are prepared to read below the surface. Allegory, analogy and metaphor were the norm, and the more repressive the régime of the time, the more heavily disguised the message had to be.

The censor — most notoriously Count Benckendorff under Nicholas I — often suspected that dangerous questions were being planted in the minds of readers and playgoers, but could usually prove neither direct criticism of the authorities, nor incitement to revolt. (Generally, the writers only got into trouble if they mixed too visibly with the political agitators.)

Early in the century, Alexander Pushkin wrote a superb narrative poem, *The Bronze Horseman*, with an allegory so finely balanced that discussion still goes on: should we read the story as a warning to stay in our allotted places in society, and never to question those in authority? Or is the tale an indictment of the despot, and the violence with which righteous rebellion is crushed?

The two central characters are Peter the Great and a minor clerk — a *tchinóvnik** — called Yevgenii.

The poem opens with a *paean* to Peter the Great, the man of vision who sought to modernise Russia, and 'break a window into Europe' by constructing a seaport on the Baltic, making it his new capital, and incidentally giving it his name.

We jump a century to a description of St Petersburg (the city he built) and the inclement weather that makes life a misery for its poorer denizens — including 'My poor, poor Yevgenii'. (It is taken for granted that the reader knows of the thousands of even more wretched souls — the slave labourers who perished in the city's construction.)

Yevgenii's dreams are more prosaic than Peter's, and they are all thwarted by his poverty and humble rank. Late one night, wandering the streets and bridges in a fever, he confronts in the moonlight the Bronze Horseman — the equestrian statue of Peter at the heart of the city. He shakes his fist at the statue, and calls out a challenge — roughly translatable as 'Up yours, Superman!'

The statue — horse and rider — seems to come to life and pursue Yevgenii through the streets. His body is found next morning in the icy waters of the Neva delta.

Yevgenii was confused, tortured and ultimately crushed by the forces of history acting upon him. We have named after him the central character in this book. We believe *our* Yevgenii is more of a survivor.

OUR YEVGENII — CHILD OF THE COLD WAR

The Russian you are going to do business with sees and hears the world through a set of filters, just as you do — but they are different filters. The filters are put there by experience. To understand others — their perceptions and their actions — we must know something of their experience.

---

*The *tchin* was the bureaucratic apparatus, organised on quasi-military lines, through which the Tsar maintained control of his empire.

We have thought about the experience of Yevgenii Mikhailovich Ivanov, born in Nizhnii Novgorod (Gor'ky) 29 March 1950. He is a composite, representing the sort of person you might get to know during a protracted negotiation or project. A decent, intelligent, family man, with limited experience of the ways of Western business people.

He was a baby under Stalin and a child under Khruschev. He was a student under Brezhnev, did his military service under Brezhnev, started his career under Brezhnev. As an adult, he has seen *uskorenie*, *glasnost'*, *perestroika*, *demokratizatsiya**, débacle in Afghanistan, the breakup of empire, the fall of Communism, chaos in the economy and crime in the streets.

Yevgenii Mikhailovich is surviving relatively well. He is virtually irreplaceable as Production Director of the factory, and the products he makes are sellable. There are hopes of foreign investment in plant, product design, distribution and marketing. His wife is a doctor, and his daughter a student of languages and business.

Yevgenii will appear as a reference point from time to time in these pages: his feelings as a youngster about the cosmonaut programme; his favourite books (including Pushkin's *Bronze Horseman*); the language he uses and how it is changing; how he gives and receives gifts; his attitude to The West; how we should address him; his schooling; his home; his style in negotiation; his collection of American popular music; his patriotism; his response to authority; the company he keeps and his style of hospitality.

His complete life story is obviously not here, nor is there any deep psychological analysis. For that, read one of the great Russian novels.

---

* *acceleration, openness, reconstruction, democratisation.*

PART ONE

Preparations

The visa is being organised for your business trip to Russia. Before departure, find a little time to lay the foundations of your model – a few facts, and some speculation.

- We begin with some handy hints on the Russian language, then come notes to give a Sense of Place and a Sense of History.
- After that, some thoughts on how it can be for a Westerner working with Russians – the kind of insights you might garner from the Old Russia Hand along the corridor.
- Then advice on what to pack for your trip – gifts, clothes, survival kit – and some suggestions about the sort of Russian music you might listen to while you pack.

1

Language

АЗБУКА — AN ALPHABET PRIMER

- It's called 'Cyrillic', after one of two Greek brothers — Kyril and Methodius — who developed it to suit the language they found spoken in Russia in the 9th century, when they were missionaries there. That's why some of the shapes are so close to the Greek alphabet.
- 33 letters — the usual vowels and consonants plus things called the soft sign and the hard sign.

Similar letter with similar sound

Some of the vowels look just the same as the Roman/English equivalents:

А О

and so do some of the consonants:

К М and **Т**

So guess what this says:

ТОМ КАТ

Soft vowels

The **E** is a *soft* vowel; it sounds as if there is a 'y' before it, or as if the consonant has gone 'soft'. ТЕМА (theme) sounds like TyEMA.

Other softening vowels are

ю = yu

As in Юрий Гагарин — YURII GAGARIN

и = ee

So МИНИ-ЮБКА is MINI-YUBKA (*mini-skirt*), and

я = ya

In Feb '45, FDR, Winnie and Uncle Joe met in ЯЛТА — YALTA

ё = yo

Which is the last vowel in ГОРБАЧЁВ — GORBACHOV

The rest of the vowels

The other vowels look strange but behave normally:

ы = i

КРЫМ is KRIM — the Crimea

э = e

ЭНЕРГИЯ = ENERGIYA; БИГ БЭН = BIG BEN

And one looks familiar, but means something different:

у = u, or oo

making LULU come out as ЛУЛУ

Consonants — the simple ones

Some look familiar, but produce different noises:

в = v

ВЬЕТ НАМ = VIET NAM

from which you can deduce that

н = n

НОРМА is NORMA, meaning "standard". That introduces us to

р = r

and there it is in the middle of СПОРТ — SPORT, which brings in

с = s

(for САША — SASHA)

and one that looks rather un-Latin, but is surely recognisable from school geometry lessons:

п = p

ПЁТР = PYOTR (Peter)

Also with obvious Greek bloodlines,

ф = f

and is in the middle of ТЕЛЕФОН — TELEFON.

Consonants — the compound sounds

Some Russian consonants combine sounds that take several letters to write out in Latin / English

ц = ts

appearing twice in ЦАРИЦА — TSARITSA (tsarina)

ч = ch

So ЧЕЧЕН = CHECHEN

ш = sh

ШШ is SHSH!, and in handwriting looks like a barbed wire entanglement.

and

щ = shch

which appears in ХРУЩЁВ — KHRUSHCHEV.

The exotic-looking

ж = zh

sounds like the French Georges, and is there in ЖИГУЛИ — ZHIGULI, the Russian name for a Lada car.

There is a guttural, like the Scottish or German throat-clearing sound:

х = kh

Giving ХОРОШО! for KHOROSHO! — GOOD!

Consonants — more unfamiliar shapes

б = b

БАБУШКА = BABUSHKA — the omnipresent *grandmother*, and БАБА ЯГА is BABA YAGA — the cannibalistic ogress of folklore.

г = g

ГРОМ = GROM — the lovely word for thunder

д = d

So ДОН is the River DON

л = l

and ЛОНДОН is LONDON.

The ninth, not the last, letter of the alphabet is

з = z

not too hard to recognise in ЗООПАРК — ZOOPARK (the collection of animals, and also a well known rock band).

The extra bits

There is 'short ee', which appears as

й

If you put it after another vowel, it bends the end of the vowel, as the English 'y' does to the 'o' in 'boy'.

So ЧАЙ is CHAY (*tea*), and ТОЛСТОЙ is TOLSTOY.

The 'soft sign' looks like this:

ь

If you find it after a consonant, it makes the consonant sound slithery and buzzy — it *softens* the consonant. Often in transliteration it shows as an apostrophe — ПЯТЬ = PYAT' (five); the novelist ГОГОЛЬ — GOGOL' had a *soft* L at the end of his name (achieved by putting the tip of your tongue on the soft part of your palate).

This only leaves

ъ

which is known as the 'hard sign'. It was used until the Revolution to show that a terminal consonant was hard and not soft. The Bolsheviks decided it was unnecessary and scrapped it — unless a consonant was shown to be soft, it was assumed to be hard. So Gogol's play *The Government Inspector* was originally РЕВИЗОРЪ (REVIZOR) and is now just spelt as РЕВИЗОР.

In the days of *perestróika*, a business magazine called КОММЕРСАНТЪ was launched — KOMMERSANT, or

Businessman. The 'hard sign' at the end of the word was a signal: 'We know this is unnecessary, but the Bolsheviks are finished, so we can do as we like'. The Ъ became the logo of the company that owned *Kommersant*.

Exercise

Write these in Russian:

KOMET (*comet*)	ROSTOV (*Rostov*)
KAMION (*truck*)	SIR (*cheese*)
ROT (*mouth*)	PTEETSA (*bird*)
SLON (*elephant*)	ZHYOLTIY DIM (*yellow smoke*)
SLADKAYA GRUSHA (*a sweet pear*)	SLEDUYUSHCHIKH CHETVERGOV (*of the following Thursdays*)
MITYA (*Micky*)	EKSKAVATORSHCHIK (*excavator operator*)

VOWELS

Familiar

А а	A
О о	O

Soft

Е е	E (ye)
Ю ю	YU
И и	EE
Я я	YA
Ё ё	YO

Hard

Ы ы	I
Э э	E
У у	U/OO

EXTRA BITS

Й й	Short EE
Ь ь	Soft Sign
Ъ ъ	Hard Sign

CONSONANTS

Familiar

К к	K
М м	M
Т т/*m**	K

Simple

В в	B
Н н	N
Р р	R
С с	S
П п	P
Ф ф	F

Compound

Ц ц	TS
Ч ч	CH
Ш ш	SH
Щ щ	SHCH
Ж ж	ZH
Х х	KH

Exotic shapes

Б б	B
Г г/*г**	G
Д д/*g**	D
Л л	L
З з	Z

---

*manuscript alternatives

PRONUNCIATION — HOW RUSSIAN SOUNDS

If you had never heard a word of spoken Russian, the alphabet would give you some clues to the dominant sounds in a Slavic language.

There is a lot of *sh...ch...kh...zh.* (There is less *ts...dz...* than in Polish, which is also more nasal than Russian.) The soft vowels prepare us for the *nye...zya...tyu...* sounds. (More in Russian than in Ukrainian or Bulgarian, where we hear more *ne...za...tu...*).

The language is intrinsically rhythmical, with much of the meaning carried by stress and intonation.

Taking these three elements together, a comedian in the West who wants to 'sound like a Russian' can string together lots of nonsense syllables — *khyuzhenyakhodeesky gryechnyekoff plyushchedzhinokh!* — and deliver them with dramatic emphasis in quite arbitrary places. Michael Bentine, a friend of Peter Sellers, was a genius at this.

Stressed and unstressed vowels

Some languages — Hungarian for example — always give full value to the vowels; every syllable in a word is pronounced, with the *a*, the *e* or the *o sounding* like *a*, *e*, or *o*.

In English, we swallow the unstressed syllables, and give out a little grunt: 'I was at a party' comes out as 'I wuzutuparty'.

Russian goes further. In any word, there is only *one* stressed syllable, and that is the only vowel that is fully pronounced. All the others slip into shadier, half-hearted versions of themselves.

ЖЕНА is ZHENA — *wife*. The stress is on the A (shown in a helpful dictionary as жена́), so the E fades from *YE* to a faint *i* sound — ZHiNA.

An unstressed Я (YA) slips into a weak *EE* sound, so ЯЗЫК (YAZIK — *language*) sounds more like eeZIK.

O is a very full and rounded sound — if it is in the stressed syllable. Otherwise, it sounds more like an *A*.

ПОТОЛОК is POTOLOK — *ceiling*. The stress is on the final O (shown in the dictionary as потоло́к), so the first two O's fade to a faint *a* sound — PaTaLOK.

The sights of a city are called ДОСТОПРИМЕЧА́ТЕЛЬНОСТИ. The accent over the A tells you that all the other syllables fade:

DaSTaPRiMiCHATiL'NaSTi

One more note on pronunciation and stress: the letter Ё (YO) is always in the stressed syllable. The battleship ПОТЁМКИН is pronounced PaTYOMKiN.

Voiced and Unvoiced Consonants

In any language, the *voiced* consonants are the ones where you have your voice-box switched on. Put your fingertips lightly on your throat and say *vvvvvvvv* or *zzzzzzzz*. You can feel your vocal chords vibrating.

Now try the same with *fffffffff* and *sssssssss*. No vibration — an *unvoiced* consonant.

VOICED	UNVOICED
Б — B	П — P
В — V	Ф — F
Г — G	К — K
Д — D	Т — T
Ж — ZH	Ш — SH
З — Z	С — S
/	Ч — CH
/	Ц — TS
/	Щ — SHCH
/	Х — KH

You can't very easily pronounce a voiced and an unvoiced consonant together as a pair. In English, we say *cubboard* rather than *cupboard* — a *voiced B* replacing the *unvoiced P*.

In Russian, if there is a pair, or a string of consonants, they often change each other from voiced to unvoiced.

ЧУВСТВО — CHUVSTVO (*feeling*) has a consonant string in the middle. When Russians say it, the first V-sound is changed to an unvoiced F- sound by the action of the letters that come after. So it is pronounced CHUFSTVa.

For the technically minded: that process is called *regressive assimilation*.

The other time that voiced consonants commonly change to unvoiced is at the end of a word. The same sort of thing happens in German, where we hear *ER HAT* for *ER HAD*.

In Russian, КРУГ — KRUG (*circle*) is pronounced more like KRUK.

That is why some newspapers opted for the spelling Gorbachoff .

And of course, we have

СМИРНОВ >> SMIRNOV >> SMIRNOFF

GRAMMAR

Russian seems to have an awful lot of grammar, and there are forests of irregularities. Studying the language at secondary school, in England in the 1960s, your author learned to stifle his sighs at the last section of each chapter of the grammar book: *So far we have covered x, y and z ... Here is a table of common exceptions to the rule...*

English grammar depends largely on word order. *Romeo loves Juliet* makes it clear who is doing the loving. *Juliet loves Romeo* is a different statement. ('Dog Bites Man' is not a news story; 'Man Bites Dog' is.)

In Russian, rather as in Latin, you are quite free to move words around in the sentence, because the relationships between the words are made clear by the twiddly bits on the ends of the words.

This is called an *inflected* language; the twiddly bits are called *inflexions*.

In the first couplet of *The Bronze Horseman*, Pushkin shows us the empty banks of the River Neva, with Peter the Great thinking his great thoughts.

The basic sentence is

HE STOOD, FULL OF GREAT THOUGHTS

To make it fit the rhythm of the line, and rhyme with the line before, Pushkin re-organises things:

СТОЯЛ ОН, ДУМ ВЕЛИКИХ ПОЛН

STOOD HE, OF THOUGHTS GREAT FULL

and it sounds just fine.

Gender

There are three — masculine, feminine and neuter.

- ДОМ — DOM (*house*) is masculine — like most nouns ending in a consonant
  (ЧЕЛОВЕК is *man*; БОГ is God)
- КНИГА — KNIGA (*book*) is feminine — like most nouns ending in A
  (ДЕВОЧКА is *girl*; РОДИНА is *Motherland*)
- ОЗЕРО — OZERO (*lake*) is neuter — like most nouns ending in O
  (ОКНО is *window*; ДЕРЕВО is *tree*)

There are many exceptions. Some nouns look like one gender, but behave like another. Just like some people we know.

Adjectives 'agree with' the noun they are attached to. Generally,

- -ЫЙ — IY is the masculine ending
- -АЯ — AYA is the feminine
- -ОЕ — OYE is the neuter

  БЕЛЫЙ ДОМ is *The White House*
  МАЛЕНЬКАЯ ЧЁРНАЯ КНИГА is *a little black book*
  ГЛУБОКОЕ ОЗЕРО is *a deep lake*.

In the plural, masculine and feminine nouns have the same ending — Ы or -И. Neutral nouns show they are plural with an -A.

Plural adjectives end in -ые or -ие:

- БЕЛЫЕ НОЧИ are the *White Nights* over St Petersburg
- ВЕЛИКИЕ ОЗЕРА are *The Great Lakes* in North America

Cases and Declensions

Nouns and adjectives decline; they change their endings for special uses. (Verbs do similar things, but are said to conjugate — of which more in a moment.) Again, just like Latin.

In ПУШКИН ПИСАЛ ПОЭМУ (*Pushkin wrote a poem*), the feminine ПОЭМА has an *accusative* ending, showing it is the object of Pushkin's action.

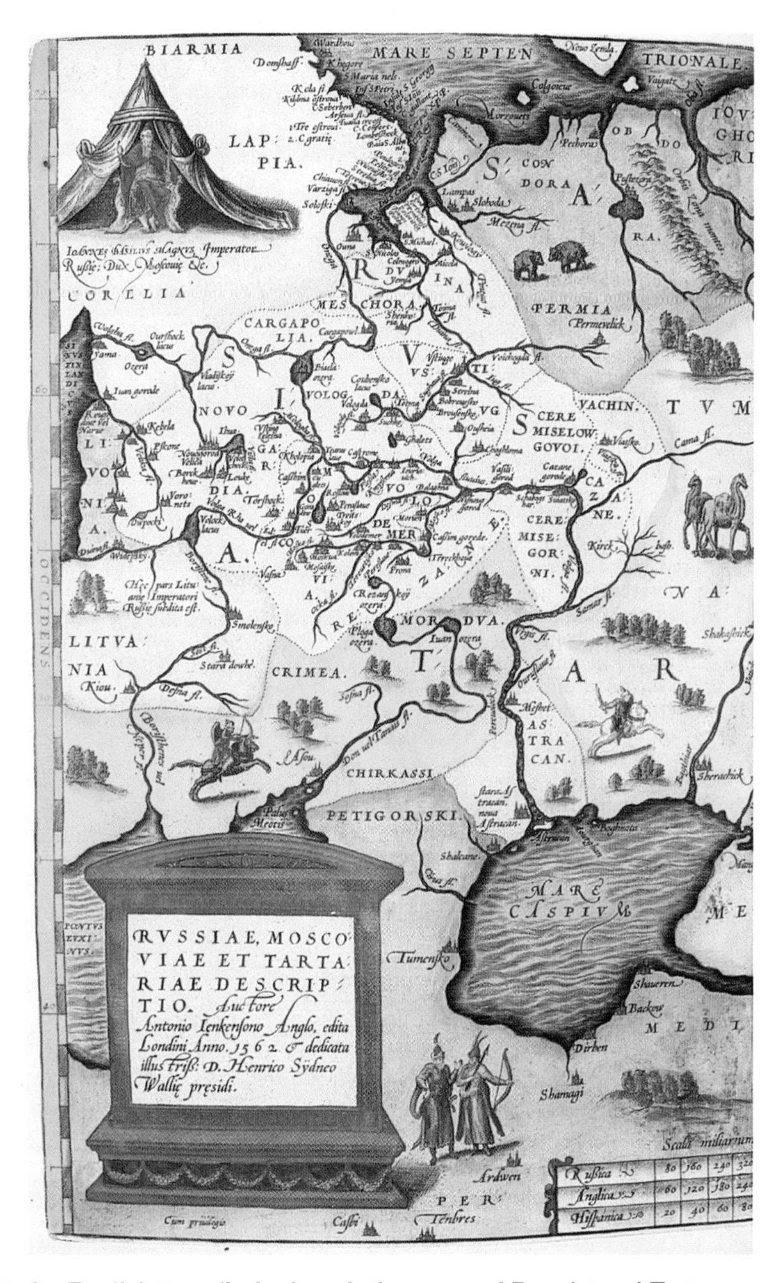

1. An English traveller's descriptive map of Russia and Tartary, 1562 (detail).

Great rivers draining into the Black Sea, the Caspian, the Baltic and the White Sea, their headwaters almost meeting: natural trade routes. Towns grew up along the rivers. (See "A sense of place: topography").

2. Ikon of the Blessed Virgin with Three Hands, Novgorod School, 16th century.

Although contemporaneous with the Renaissance, such images show little influence from Italy. (See “A sense of history: religion; isolation”).

The third hand commemorates a 7th-century priest in Constantinople, whose amputated hand grew back through the Virgin’s intercession.

3. "In the Birch Tree Forest", I. Siskin, late 19th century – when there were strong Western influences in Russian art and ideas.

The traditional word for countryside is *derévnya*, derived from *dérevo* – tree. The ancient spirit of *Rus* lives in the forest (See "Views from your car seat: countryside").

1.
КРЕСТЬЯНИН СМОТРИ НА
КАРТИНУ ЭТУ: ПОЙМЕШЬ ПОЧЕМУ
ВЗДОРОЖАЛИ БИЛЕТЫ
2.
ТРАНСПОРТ РАЗРУШЕН-НАСТОЯ
ЩИЙ ТРУП СВИСТНУТЬ ПАРОВОЗУ
СТОИТ РУБЛЬ
3.
А ЕЗДЯТ ВСЕ КОМУ НЕ ЛЕНЬ
ЕЗДЯТ НОЧЬ ЕЗДЯТ ДЕНЬ
КАССА
4.
ВОЛНЕ ЛЮДСКОЙ НЕ ВИДАТЬ
КОНЦА. А ВЕЗЕТ С СОБОЙ
ПОЛТОРА ОГУРЦА
5.
ЕЗДИТ ПАРОВОЗ-ОТДЫХУ
НИ МИНУТКИ.
50 коп
6.
А В КАССЕ-ПОЛТИННИК ЗА ЦЕЛЫЕ
СУТКИ

4. Railway poster, V. Mayakovsky, early 1920s (Detail).

Futurism, and the *avant-garde* in general, flourished under the Bolsheviks in the liberal 1920s – alongside the New Economic Policy (See "A sense of history: swings").

Here the dynamic style delivers a lesson in economics to the railway traveller.

1. Peasant, look at this picture: this is why tickets have got dearer.
2. The transport's a total wreck. Each blast of the whistle costs a rouble.
3. But anyone who feels like it takes a ride, by day and by night.
4. You can't see the end of the queue – just to transport half a cucumber.
5. So the poor loco works without a minute's rest.
6. The cashier has only taken half a rouble all day.

5. "The first five-year plan: a morning scene", Y. Romas, early 1930s.

Under Stalin, the official style flourished in art and literature – Socialist Realism praising the party, its policies and, of course, its leader.

The style often celebrated the cult of bigness – a recurrent theme in Russian public works since the first tsars (See: "A sense of place: scale").

6. "Alexander Nevsky", P. Korin, early 1940s.

In the Great Patriotic War, Stalin invoked the 13th-century hero-prince-saint of Novgorod, in his call-to-arms against the Hitlerites.

Nevsky's facial expression exemplifies the wary Russian attitude to foreigners (See "Yevgenii Mikhailovich: National pride; the world outside").

7. Front page of *Krokodil* magazine, early 1950s.

The word *MIR* on the marcher's tunic means both *WORLD* and *PEACE*.

Russians who grew up in this period, exposed to propaganda like this, find it difficult to believe that Russia was feared in the West as a dangerous war threat (See "Yevgenii Mikhailovich: early years").

Younger Russians find such images mawkish and hypocritical.

8. Portrait of artist friends, by A. Gerasimov, 1960s.

This painting captures a timeless Russian ideal of convivial but earnest conversation, with the essential accoutrements to hand. Whatever his background, you can expect your Russian business partner to hold views on artistic and literary matters (See "Negotiation: celebrating", and "Yevgenii at home").

Some other cases:

СТОЛ = TABLE	НА СТОЛЕ = ON THE TABLE
БРАТ= BROTHER	БРАТА = BROTHER'S/OF THE BROTHER
МОЛОТОК = HAMMER	МОЛОТКОМ = WITH A HAMMER

And the adjectives go along with the nouns:

В МАЛЕНЬКОЙ ЧЁРНОЙ КНИГЕ, БЕЛЫМ КАРАНДАШОМ
= IN THE LITTLE BLACK BOOK, WITH A WHITE PENCIL

One further note about nouns: there are no definite or indefinite articles (*a...an...the*) in Russian. So you just have to feel your way — perhaps this last phrase should really be translated as IN A LITTLE BLACK BOOK WITH THE WHITE PENCIL.

Pronouns, Possessive Adjectives and the like

ОНА ВЗЯЛА СВОЮ РУЧКУ И МОЮ БУМАГУ И НАПИСАЛА ЕМУ ПИСЬМО = SHE TOOK HER OWN PEN AND MY PAPER AND WROTE HIM A LETTER

You just have to learn the tables, to be found at the front of any pocket dictionary. The entry price to the Russian language is high.

Verbs

In the past tense, verbs change according to the gender of the subject.

Pushkin *napisál* a poem. Anna Akhmatova *napisála* her verse.

In the present and the future, the verb is more interested in whether it's me, you, him/her/it or them doing the action. *I work*, but *she works*. Most languages do this kind of conjugation.

Here's a regular example:

Я работаю I work	Мы работаем we work
Ты работаешь you work (*familiar*)	Вы работаете you work (*plural/polite*)
Он работает he works	Они работают they work

There are lots of variations, but generally a Ю — YU ending means 'I do this' (*Slushayu!* — I'm listening!):

-Ю — YU	= I...	-M — M	= WE...
-ШЬ — SH	= YOU...	-TE — TYE	= YOU...
-T — T	= HE/ SHE/ IT	-ЯТ/-ЮТ — YAT/ YUT	= THEY...

There is a collection of prefixes which enrich the meaning of verbs:

- РВАТЬ — RVAT' means TO TEAR.
- ОТОРВАТЬ — OTORVAT' means TO TEAR OFF.
- ВЫРВАТЬ — VIRVAT' means TO TEAR OUT, WRENCH OR SNATCH.
- РАЗОРВАТЬ — RAZORVAT' means TO TEAR UP INTO PIECES.
- РАЗОРВАТЬСЯ — RAZORVAT'SYA (reflexive) means TO EXPLODE.

The really exotic thing about Russian verbs is that each one exists in two aspects, the *perfective* and the *imperfective*. So there are two infinitives for each verb, (КОНЧАТЬ/КОНЧИТЬ — KONCHAT'/ KONCHIT' — to finish) and you use one for the future, and a different one for repeated actions in the future, or if you want to suggest in the past that one action was about to be interrupted by another.

In 1972, your author took a good Honours Degree in Russian language, literature, geography, history and so on, at a reputable English university. He passed his final examination without ever having mastered the perfective-imperfective game — constructing his sentences so as to avoid the problem.

The Russians take it with their mothers' milk. Here we leave Russian grammar.

2

A Sense of Place

TOPOGRAPHY

Rivers

> *"Even today, to the confusion of strangers, the people of Russia have difficulty in giving directions. Ask if a road runs east or west, north or south, and a Russian will not know. Why should he, in that endless landscape, where horizon succeeds horizon, always the same?*
>
> *But he can tell you how the rivers run."*
>
> Edward Rutherfurd, *Russka* (a saga-novel)

The great rivers of Russia — the Volga, Dnieper, Don and Dniester — were the original North–South thoroughfares. Linked to the Baltic river system by portage and haulage (before the canals), they brought the Viking trade and the first rulers of Kievan *Rus*. Broad and navigable to the Black Sea and the Caspian, they exported furs and slaves and gave access to the trade routes that ran East–West from the Mediterranean to China: spices, silks, and the Christian religion.

Steppe

Once the grazing ground of migratory deer, and the home of nomads renowned for their horsemanship. The Russian part of the great Euro-Asian prairie.

There is a North–South graduation: Mixed Forest...Forest/Steppe... True Steppe...Semi-Desert. The middle swathe of this is the *Chernozem* — the Black Earth — where, natives say, you can thrust a stick into the ground and come back later for a harvest.

The larder of Russia, depleted in parts by the action of the wind, and of man — particularly badly managed irrigation schemes which have eroded and leached the soil.

Taiga (*taigá*)

The Russian word for countryside is *derévnya.* It comes from the same stem as *dérevo*, meaning tree.

> “*...the Siberian forest, the taiga, thickened, blurring the distant hills with smudges of trees and hiding the settlements that had swallowed so many banished Russians...*”
>
> Paul Theroux, *The Great Railway Bazaar*

The largest coniferous forest in the world, home to wolf, bear and mink.

Tundra

North of the forests, the frozen wastes — up to nine months below freezing, with permanently frozen subsoil (permafrost). Lichens, some grasses and dwarf shrubs. Reindeer and birds.

The mineral wealth below the surface has brought man and his machines to the tundra, and their waste products are upsetting the fragile eco-balance.

CLIMATE

The classic *continental climate* — a huge landmass whose centre cannot benefit from the moderating effects of surrounding temperate seas (as Britain does, for example). This brings extremes of temperature between the seasons.

With the break-up of the Soviet Union, Russia retained the northern parts, while secessionist republics have taken back the sunshine belt and the deserts. Russia has kept the cold bits.

It is commonly said that Napoleon and Hitler were defeated by ‘General Winter’.

The summer is fairly short, but reliable, and Russians greet it wholeheartedly. In August, the squares of the more prosperous towns are full of caterers, entertainers and promenading families.

SCALE

Quiz

1. **Area**. The Russian Federation covers :
   a) 2 million Sq km — like 50 Denmarks.
   b) 17 million Sq km — like 200 Portugals.
   c) 9 million Sq km — like 56,000 Liechtensteins

2. **The Volga** rises in the Valdai Hills, and flows to the Caspian. It is personified as *mat' reká — mother river* in the Song of the Volga Boatmen. It fits easily into the Central European part of Russia. How long is it?
   a) 1947 km — like the distance from Rome to Berlin.
   b) 3531 km — like the distance from Aberdeen to Gibraltar.
   c) 3117 km — like the distance from Paris to Istanbul.

3. **Kamchatka** is a volcanic corner of Russia. It has
   a) an active volcano.
   b) 100 active volcanoes.
   c) 10 active volcanoes.

4. **Time Zones.**You are having mid-morning coffee in St Petersburg, when your telephone rings. The caller says 'Good morning, I'm calling from Petropavlovsk-Kamchatskiy'. Do you say,
   a) Good morning (like London to Stockholm)
   b) Good evening (like Hawaii to Dublin)
   c) Good afternoon (like Rome to Delhi) ?

5. **Climate.** At Oymyakon, in Eastern Siberia, the lowest temperature recorded is
   a) –32° Celsius.
   b) –67° Celsius.
   c) –44° Celsius.

6. **Economy.** The turbulence triggered by *perestroika* produced inflation. In 1992, prices in the Russian Federation rose
   a) by 750 per cent.
   b) by 2500 per cent.
   c) by 1800 per cent.

7. **Resources.** Russia is estimated to possess
   a) 15% of the world's coal reserves,
   b) Half the world's coal reserves,
   c) 30% of the world's coal reserves,

not to mention iron ore, uranium, zinc, manganese, diamonds, mercury, copper, gold, oil, gas, timber, HEP, fish, game, scenery, a highly educated population...

Answers

In every case, the answer is **b.**

Russians think big — big music, big ballet, big books. They build 5000-bed hotels. In the Virgin Lands campaign, between 1953 and 1956, 80 million acres were brought under cultivation for the first time. More Russians than Americans believe it might be feasible to control the weather — and the Central Aerological Observatory was offering to do just that in 1995: for a $20,000 fee, they would seed the clouds around Moscow and ensure clear skies for the Victory Day celebrations — which were BIG....

Some say that this overriding passion for quantity has a bad effect on Russian attitudes to quality.

THE PEOPLES

- Official population estimate 1991: 148,485,000.
- Russians make up 82%, Tartars 4%, Ukrainians 3%, Belorussians 1%. As a legacy of Empire, the remaining 10% is made up of some 115 ethnic groups, ranged under the headings: Western, South and Eastern Slavs, Baltic Peoples, Armenians, Georgians, Turkic Peoples, Iranian peoples, Peoples of the North, Moldovans, Germans, Gypsies.
- In 1897, there were 5 million Jews in Russia. In 1989, 1.45 million.

THE THREE RUSSIAS

The Tsar was 'Emperor of All the Russias' — Great Russia (= Russia), Little Russia (= Ukraine) and White Russia (= Belarus).

Ukraine

- 233,000 square miles — 2.7% of the old Soviet Union.
- Population 52 million — 73% Ukrainian, 22% Russian.
- Major resources: food (grain, potatoes, beet) and coal (the Donbass field).

The original *RUS* — Kievan Russia. As much the subject of archaeology as of history, since it was a pre-literate society during much of its development. The version of its growth given in *The Russian Primary Chronicle* (late 12th century) is naturally suspect.

Nor do we really know how its people came to see themselves as distinct from the Great Russians. There were Varangians, Khazars, Finns and Tatars spread over the whole area, and integrated into the Russian identity.

Ryurik ruled Kiev from 860; Vladimir I imposed conversion to Byzantine Orthodox Christianity from 989; Yaroslav the Wise, two Svyatopolks, a Vsevolod, and Vladimir Monomakh ruled through good and troubled times until 1240, when the Mongol conquest was completed.

Fought for independence 1917–21. Lost, and was in the USSR thereafter.

Bears the brunt of the Chernobyl disaster. Owns a good part of the Black Sea coast — a source of woe to many Russians, whose holidays there had long seemed a natural right.

Tension with the Russians? A joke from the early cosmonaut days:

> **Ukrainian I:** The Russians have gone into space!
> **Ukrainian 2** (very excited): What — all of them?

Belarus (formerly Belorussia)

- 80,000 square miles — 0.9% of old Soviet territory.
- Population 10.2 million — 3.5% of former USSR: 78% Belorussian, 13% Russian, 4% Polish.
- Major resources: food (meat, dairy, mixed farming — much land unusable since Chernobyl)) and sophisticated industry (electronics, machine tools, consumer goods).

It was once said that a King of England who stood at a high window of Windsor Castle and looked East along the Thames would see no higher land between him and the Urals. His gaze would travel across Belarus — White Russia.

At times in the last thousand years, a shifting border with Lithuania and with Poland. Capital in Minsk.

Across this land — the Western Marches — the Russians fell back before the Grande Armée and the Wehrmacht, stretching and harrying their lines of communication. In this land the invaders faced the White Russian winter. The White Russian people suffered appallingly: 2,230,000 dead 1941–45.

Belorussia was always closely tied to the centre of the Soviet economy — importing energy (90 per cent) and raw materials (70 per cent), and exporting its products back into the system, military output playing a vital role.

Great Russia (as it is still known on ceremonial occasions)

Centre of the Soviet empire

For generations, the world outside used 'Russia' as shorthand for 'The Soviet Union'.* Gorbachev once annoyed Belorussians and Ukrainians by making the same slip in a speech.

Stalin shelved the Internationalist idea of world communism, and built a Russo-centric communist empire, with Moscow at the hub.

Growth of Muscovy

Moscow was first prominent in 1147, and grew in power over the centuries. In 1310 Moscow became See of the Orthodox Church, in 1380 Prince Dmitri defeated the Golden Horde, and a century later Mongol dominance was over.

Novgorod, Viatka, Pskov, Riazan and Smolensk came under Moscow's sway by 1533. Ivan IV ('the Terrible') was crowned Tsar, and annexed Kazan, Astrakhan and the Mongols East of the Urals.

Muscovite Russia and The Ukraine expanded west into Polish lands in the seventeenth century.

The settlement of Siberia and the Far East was gradual until the 1700s, by which time there were 200,000 Russians living east of the Urals — dotted about among the water systems of the Yenisei (3600 miles) and the Lena (2550 miles), the Pamir, Tien Shan and Altai mountain ranges, and the Kamchatka peninsula out into the Pacific.

The South, with turbulent Cossacks (originally peasants and paupers fleeing economic and religious oppression), and the tribes of the Caucasus to contend with, has always been a trouble to Russia, but has been important for access to warm seas and, latterly, to oil.

---

*In the same way, Russians generally use *Anglia* to denote the whole of Great Britain. In the late 60s, Kosygin and his interpreter slipped up on this, and delighted the Scottish nationalists by apparently embracing the cause of Scottish separatism.

Homo sovieticus spoke Russian

From Moscow, the Soviet empire was run on monocultural lines — compulsory Russian at school for all children, Russians at the heads of ministries, predominantly Russian officers in the multi-racial Red Army. Citizens of other states and republics married Russians, came to Moscow to seek justice when they could not find it at home, tried to find ways to wangle a Moscow resident's permit — for better career prospects, access to better shops, exposure to cosmopolitan ideas.

The *Cambridge Encyclopedia of Russia* offers this on monoculturalism:

> "*A good example of this unthinking chauvinism was the renaming of the Kyrgyz capital, Bishkek, after the Red Army general Frunze. This ... entirely ignored the fact that there is no* f *sound in Kyrgyz!*"

In the 1970s the plastics industry in the Soviet Union and its satellites was held together by an industrial association which met annually to discuss technical and logistical matters — and also to enjoy the social aspects of the *komandiróvka* (business trip / junket).

The conference rotated around the capital cities of the empire, with Budapest no doubt proving more popular than Bucharest. The rota was organised alphabetically by the name of the country — the *Russian* name of the country, in *Russian* alphabetical order. In Hungarian, that country is called *Magyarország*, but in Russian it is *Vengria*, which according to Russian alphabetical order places it before *Estonia*.

The Hungarian plastics engineer who gave me this story treasured it as an example of the insidious, niggling Russian colonialism that exasperated the peoples of the satellites — even the Hungarians, with their 'goulash communism' and relatively high standard of living.

That exasperation, amplified through millions of lives in three generations, sped the collapse of the Soviet empire.

In 1990, a student from Byelorussia commented on that disintegration:

> "*Assuming that by my early thirties I have not been killed in a civil war, I think what will be left will be Russia — the original core territory. And that is what happened to the Roman Empire, isn't it? It shrank. I just hope it all happens without haste, and peacefully.*"
>
> quoted in David Remnick, *Lenin's Tomb*

Igor's prediction has been proved accurate. His hope has proved empty.

3

A Sense of History

THE YOKE

"The new has been welcomed in America, the old has been revered in Russia."

Yale Richmond, *From NYET to DA: Understanding the Russians*

"Not every headache in Russian business can be attributed to our communist past. The dynamic between entrepreneurial initiative on the one hand, and repressive and autocratic ruling systems on the other, between the individual and the state, goes much further back."

Vladimir Kvint, *The Barefoot Shoemaker*

"If the people are not kept in great dread they will never obey the laws. As a horse without a bridle is under its rider, so is a kingdom without dread under its king."

Ivan Peresvetov, *In the time of Ivan IV*

The history of Russia can be read as a story of oppression and the casting off of oppression.

The Tatar Yoke

From 1240 to 1480, the Tatars exacted a tough tribute from vassal Russia, and they remained a terrible nuisance until Catherine the Great conquered the Crimea three hundred years after that.

The Golden Horde were vindictive overlords, capable of great arbitrary cruelty.

"They learn warfare from their youth...they are stern, fearless and fierce towards us...We cannot oppose them, but humiliate ourselves before them, as Jacob did before Esau."

A Russian monk of the time

Between 1240 and 1480, the European Renaissance was changing people's view of the world. Beneath the Tatar yoke, Russia experienced none of it.

The Tsarist Yoke

Ivan IV (1533–84) was eager for contact with the West, and made welcome an English sailor-explorer, Richard Chancellor. Chancellor reported Ivan's cloth-of-gold pavilion as superior to those of English and French kings.

One of the great cinema stills is from Eisenstein's 'Ivan the Terrible' — Nikolay Cherkasov in tall fur hat and a beard like a trenching tool, staring into the lens from the corners of his eyes, the corners of his mouth turned down, his brows arched. Paranoia, aggression, and a highly developed sense of his own importance.

Ivan took a large part of the country as his own property — the *opríchnina*, or 'realm apart' — ejecting landowners wholesale and enforcing his will through a reign of terror enforced by his *opríchniki*.

His name might translate better as 'Ivan the Dread', or 'Ivan the Awesome'.

Nicholas I (1825–55) was the other great repressive autocrat. Known as 'The Gendarme of Europe', he ran the country like a military camp, through an enormous system of police.

A French traveller wrote:

"The word of the Czar has the power to create, they say. Yes, it brings stones to life, but in so doing it kills men...

Everything that gives a meaning and a goal to political institutions reduces itself here to one lone sentiment—fear."

The Marquis de Custine, *Journey for Our Time*: July 1839

Although Nicholas recognised that the institution of serfdom was retarding economic and social development, he feared the turmoil that might follow any wholesale emancipation of four-fifths of the population. It was for his successor to grasp that nettle.

> *"In the Tsardom of Moscow of the sixteenth and seventeenth centuries we find an entirely new concept of society and its relation to the state. All the classes of the nation...were bound to the service of the state..."*
>
> George Vernadsky, *The Mongols and Russia*

The Bolshevik Yoke

- 'Bound to the service of the state' — as interpreted by members of the Party.
- An estimated 500,000 members of the KGB.
- Five-Year Plans, Collectivisation of Agriculture, the GULAG.
- Before the start of the Great Terror (1936–1939), the XVII Party Congress elected a Central Committee. At the end, 70 per cent of them had been executed, with or without a show trial.

The engineer of the purges was celebrated in over a thousand place names during his lifetime — Stalinsk, Stalinogorsk, Stalinabad, Stalingrad... .

EAST AND WEST

> *"The Russian is a delightful person till he tucks in his shirt. As an oriental he is charming. It is only when he insists upon being treated as the most easterly of western peoples instead of the most westerly of easterns that he becomes a racial anomaly and extremely difficult to handle."*
>
> Rudyard Kipling, *The Man Who Was*

Slavophiles and Westernisers

The East–West issue runs through all Russian history.

- When Peter the Great made his boyars shave off their beards and wear Western style breeches, it was a telling way of communicating his *political* message: 'We Westernise *now*.'
- The purpose of St Petersburg — 'to break a window into Europe' has already been noted. To be a Westerniser in *trade and industry* was to be an admirer of Adam Smith and the Industrial Revolution.
- By the nineteenth century, *the arts* was divided along the same fault line, with the Westerniser Turgenev attracting the scorn of Dostoevsky — who was a slavophile.

The slavophiles were largely the nationalist/conservative/religious lobby. They tended to be mystical where the westernisers were pragmatic, and sought to preserve Russian spiritual values — which usually went with a preference for rustic traditions and institutions. Slavophiles liked to wear big beards.

In times of turbulent change, some part of the Russian psyche returns to traditional values. Now that the state that persecuted him has crumbled, Solzhenitsyn has returned home to try to make his voice heard as a slavophile prophet.

Some see Russia's historical resistance to change, its love of stratification and ranks, and its propensity for bureaucracy as expressions of the Asian element in the ethnic mix.

RELIGION

Orthodox church

The Nordic pantheon was also worshipped in the forests of Kievan Rus — with Perun, the God of Thunder, at the top.

Byzantine Christianity was the state religion from 988, centred in Kiev, then Vladimir (late 13th–early 14th century), then Moscow. The Mongols were tolerant.

From 1200 to 1600 the monastic foundations flourished. In 1588 the English Ambassador to Moscow observed that the monasteries owned all Russia's best land.

In the early 16th century the monk Filofey propounded the idea that Moscow was to be the Third Rome (after Rome herself and Constantinople) — after which there would be no fourth.

Meanwhile the institution of *stártsy* (spiritual elders) was gathering momentum. Meek and humble, Bishop Tikhon of Zadonsk (1724–83) and Serafim of Sarov (1759–1833) were nationally revered. The fictional Father Zossima (in Dostoevsky's *Brothers Karamazov*) and the all-too real Grigory Rasputin (1869-1916) were in the *stártsy* tradition.

Different tsars evolved different contracts with the church. It never suffered serious repression until the 1920s and 1930s, when the Bolsheviks strove for universal atheism.

Stalin found it expedient in wartime to tap the church's patriotic potential, and there was a revival in Christian fortunes through to the 1950s, when Khrushchev mounted a tough anti-religious campaign.

At Easter 1995, Yeltsin announced that the Patriarch was to be given an official residence inside the Kremlin. Once again the church is accepted as repository of conservative, quintessentially Russian, values.

> *"The Russian Orthodox church, with its dark, incense filled interiors lit by the flickering light of candles and resounding to the chant of an unaccompanied choir, is the image of heaven on earth. It is not a place to sit and hear sermons about the evils of VAT on domestic heating."*
>
> Elizabeth Roberts, *Xenophobe's Guide to the Russians*

Holy destiny

Much as many Americans feel a sense of responsibility to preach 'The American Way' worldwide, so there is a thread of messianism running through Russia's national philosophy.

While the American national genius is expressed in terms of know-how, can-do, and gung-ho, the Russians claim for themselves the high spiritual ground.

Filofey and the Third Rome we have mentioned. Four centuries after him, Dostoevsky's novel *The Idiot* depicted a Russia which must pass through suffering to salvation, and then on to its messianic destiny among the world's nations.

A hundred years later again, the economist Mikhail Antonov was interviewed for the *New York Times Magazine*:

"Let other countries surpass each other in the technology of computer production...only we can provide an answer to the question: Why? For whose sake? We are the only legitimate heirs to the great, spiritual Russian culture. The saving of the world will come from Soviet Russia."

Communism

It is a truism now to say Communism is a religion, and even, arguably, that Lenin is a God.

Christianity absorbed pagan practices — placing the birth of Christ at the winter solstice and hijacking the rituals, for example. In the same way, Russian communism offered surrogate activities even as Christianity was being repressed.

Not far from Lenin's mausoleum, the most important shrine of his cult, stands the tomb of the unknown soldier — the outdoor altar to patriotism where newly-wed couples come to place the bridal bouquet. The marriage itself until recently was sanctified in the Palace of Weddings ceremony by the Soviet Socialist Motherland.

When communism imploded, into the void rushed the much-publicised quacks and charlatans. In TV-séances, they claim to cure everything from baldness to AIDS, and millions follow them. It is all part of *bogoiskatel'stvo* — the search for God.

ISOLATION

In 1839 Custine speculated that

"Russia...has been deprived of a profound fermentation and of the benefit of a slow and natural cultural development, because of the impatience of her leaders."

Renaissance? Enlightenment? Industrial revolution?

We have already observed how the Tatars denied Russia access to the Renaissance. Russian literature, art and architecture followed a separate path.

The fruits of Western Europe's Scientific Revolution in the 16th century reached Russia only as imports a hundred years later, when Peter the Great (1682–1725) undertook his Grand Embassy — an intellectual shopping trip from the court of England's King William III to the shipyards of Zaandam.

In the late 18th century, Catherine the Great (1762–96) admitted the ideas of the Enlightenment selectively — preferring the German variety, with its emphasis on the wealth and strength of the state, to the French sort, which were more socially radical. No guillotine for Catherine; it was Pugachev, the leader of a great peasant revolt in 1773–75, who lost *his* head.

The 19th-century repressiveness of Nicholas I was discussed under The Yoke (see page 43). It was not a fertile environment for an industrial revolution, or the development of liberal capitalism.

Heavy industrial expansion came in a rush in the 1890s, and peasants flooded into the cities to become wage slaves.

Martin Gilbert's *Atlas of Russian History* lists Russia's main exports in 1914: Cereals, timber, petroleum, eggs, flax, butter, sugar. The imports: Raw cotton, machinery and metal goods, tea, coal, iron, lead, copper.

The twentieth century?

Visitors at all stages of Russia's development have commented upon a strain of secretiveness in the national character, and have sought to connect it with a national sense of inferiority: we don't want to show you what we have or how we do things, in case you laugh at us.

In matters military and scientific, the explanation has been less tortuous: we don't want to show you what we have, in case you take advantage of us.

From Stalin onwards, Soviet science was sealed off from curious outsiders, and from invigorating outside influences. (The absurd results are chronicled in Solzhenitsyn's *First Circle*.)

Technical, commercial and industrial methods in the West have followed a general trend towards efficiency, economy and eco-friendliness. The Bolshevik philosophy rejected management science as bourgeois, and drew no benefit from advances in the social disciplines; the Soviet system discouraged honest feedback within itself, so excesses and vicious spirals were common; the centrally-planned economy demanded crude growth, and left no space for such delicate ideas as Total Quality Management.

"If all the raw materials that Russia produces were sold abroad, the country would earn twice as much as its present total GDP...Yet raw-material output is included in GDP. If GDP is lower, it must mean Russian industry is subtracting, not adding, value to the raw materials it consumes.... Russia would be better off if every industrial worker stopped working."

The Economist, 5 December 1992

Thirty-five miles from Norway, in the Arctic tundra, is the town of Nikel — population 15,000.

"...up to 700 square miles around Nikel are a man-made desert. Nikel emits over 250,000 tonnes of sulphur dioxide a year in the course of making 100,000 tonnes of low-grade nickel...90 per cent of Nikel's population have damaged lungs..."

John Vidal, *Guardian*, 5 November 1994

The river Kolva, in the Komi republic, suffered a disaster when an oil pipeline sprang 23 leaks.

"...estimates of the amount of oil leaked range between the Russian figure of 14,000 tonnes and the American 272,000 tonnes.... Russia's Minister for Emergencies, Sergei Shoigu, has estimated there are two oil spills a week in Russia and about 50 million tonnes leaked every year...[a local informant in Komi expresses despair].... Such hopelessness, encouraged by 70 years of totalitarianism, has been aggravated by a lifetime spent more than 700 miles away from the power in Moscow, in a sparsely-populated region where in winter the temperature drops to 40 degrees below zero and the night falls at 3 pm."

Victoria Clark, *Independent on Sunday*, 6 November 1994

During that 70 years, Western entrepreneurs refined their communications, systems of measurement, distribution networks, and financial control techniques. Not so in Russia, where to be a middle-man was to be a criminal.

Michael Kadenacy had the job of launching Baskin-Robbins ice cream in Russia — sourcing the raw materials, setting up a production plant, establishing a sales network.

> “*Most Russians live day-to-day and hope time will take care of everything; it made sense in a country where no one knew what tomorrow would bring but it means there is no long term view...[of the bureaucrats he deals with:] some are learning fast but others are rigid and stupid; sorry, arbitrary and capricious. A generation will pass before the bad old ways are forgotten...We are not here to dictate. The companies who arrive knowing it all don't stand a chance. This is no place for hot-shots.*”
>
> *Financial Times*, 8 November 1993

Censorship

Peter the Great introduced censorship; under Nicholas I, the secret police (in their sky-blue uniforms) were enthusiastic and notoriously clumsy censors; Soviet censorship started with the *Decree on the Press* (27 October 1917), which stated that 'counter-revolutionary' publications were no less dangerous than bombs and machine-guns By the 1930s, censorship applied to circuses, bus tickets, and handkerchiefs with pictures on them.

Discussion of censorship was censored. No Soviet publication mentioned the jamming of foreign radio transmissions — a measure taken to protect the people from the damaging knowledge that living standards in the West were improving, and that Marx might have got it wrong about the inevitable fall of capitalism.

To get a sense of how this control of information influenced social mores and individual initiative, read Orwell's *1984* — which was finally published in Russia in 1989, along with Solzhenitsyn's *Gulag Archipelago* and the works of Trotsky.

SWINGS

Russia's size and ethnic complexity have made it difficult to govern. When the pendulum of power has swung to an extreme of centralised control, the forces of domestic discontent, external influence or economic expediency have pulled it back. On the downswing, the pendulum has gained momentum and reform has come in a rush — destabilising institutions and frightening the next incumbent into another cycle of repression.

- **Ivan IV** (16th century): started as a *reformer,* ended as a *reactionary despot.*
- **Time of Troubles** (early 17th): *chaos* — social discontent, succession disputes, incursions by Poles and Swedes.
- **Early Romanovs** (mid-17th): restoration of internal *order.*
- **Peter the Great ... Catherine the Great** (18th): *change* — government, economic structure, social systems, foreign policy.
- **Nicholas I** (early 19th): *repression.*
- **Alexander II** (mid-19th): *emancipation* of the serfs, creation of the State Bank, elected local councils (*zemstva*). Assassinated 1881.
- **Alexander III ... Nicholas II** (late 19th): harsh *control* and rejection of liberal reforms.
- **Lenin** (1920s): *revolution*, civil war, reorganisation of everything, NEP (New Economic Policy: hybrid capitalism), temporary tolerance of intellectual and creative *freedom.*
- **Stalin** (1930s, 1940s): *autocracy*, centralisation, mass Party membership, all opposition crushed.
- **Khrushchev** (1950s): de-Stalinisation, 'golden period', some freedom of expression and *openness* to Western ideas.
- **Brezhnev** (1960s, 1970s): caution, bureaucracy, *stagnation.*
- **Andropov & Chernenko** (early 1980s): *Gerontocracy.* 'Can we go on like this?
- **Gorbachev** (late 1980s): *reconstruction*

4

Working with Russians

WHAT EXPATS SAY

It's been *seventy years* of Bolshevism here. That's critically different from Hungary's 'forty wasted years'. There is no generation alive in Russia now that can remember how things were done before — no tradition of entrepreneurship, principled negotiation, or responsible decision-making.

It happens all the time. Some enterprise — a bank or whatever — gives us a contract to audit their accounts. We find anomalies and evidence of double-dealing, so we say: 'Sorry, we're going to have to qualify your accounts, we can't approve them.' Their response: 'Bloody unhelpful Westerners!'

I've been here ten years now, and I know it's hopeless going into a meeting with a list of bullet points. It brings out the worst in them — procrastination, prevarication, obfuscation.

They have a genius for improvisation and cobbling-together. It's called nakhódchivost' *— resourcefulness. They're not pursuing excellence, they're pursuing good-enoughness. Kerosene-powered space rockets, the T-34 tank, the way they mix the cement at 30 degrees below in* ***Ivan Denisovitch****...*

> “In general the Russians manifest their intelligence rather by the manner in which they use poor tools than by the care they put into perfecting these tools.”
>
> Marquis de Custine, *Journey for Our Time*

They don't go in for contingency planning — no back-up, no Plan B.

I ran some psychometric tests on a group of Russian managers at a seminar. They came out very low on Need-Achievement.

I had to sack one — Oleg, the one bloke in a team of four who wasn't pulling his weight. He came round to my apartment that evening and said he wanted to thank me for all the things he'd learned in the six months. I told the others the next day, and they all said they would have done the same.

Motivation isn't really an issue. They're so pleased to be in a secure job with a Western company.

I've finally settled on a straightforward *nachál'nik* (boss) style. They were unhappy when I tried to get all democratic — they couldn't work out how the system of rewards and punishment would work.

Somebody called it 'learned helplessness'. Under the old system, getting ahead was virtually impossible — so they lost the habit of trying.

> "I discovered very quickly that it was necessary to scream a bit if you wanted to be taken seriously', Durham observed at the end of his first week in Moscow. 'Stand up, get in their face, and yell at them like you would a stubborn bulldog. A businesslike demeanour gets you nowhere here."
>
> A. Craig Copetas, *Bear Hunting with the Politburo*

It's the environment that demotivates them. Step One is to create a positive working environment. Step Two is to show them that you mean it.

There's a bit of devilment goes on. One of the ways they used to try and stay sane in their old jobs was to create problems in order to relieve the tedium.

It's what I call a *reaction* society, rather than a *pre-emption* society. It used to be that our HQ would airfreight components [for telephone exchanges] out to us, then they'd sit in the customs shed for a while, then the customs people would contact our office, *then* one of my staff would contact our bank and start talking about a money draft to take out to the airport to pay the duty. I said, 'get moving on the money draft as soon as the plane lands'. So they do that now.

The new assembly line keeps the workers on their toes, and we pay them good money. People come for a month to see how they like it, and if they can stand the pace, they stay on.

There is always a lack of co-ordination or continuity somewhere. The relationship between facts and ideas is hazy; calculations are merely approximate and perspectives blurred and uncertain...Russians see reality only through a mist of dreams, and never have precise notions of time or space!

Maurice Paléologue, *An Ambassador's Memoirs, 1914–1917*

Our Human Resources department came over to 'help' us with our recruitment. They wanted me to work with them on a profile of the ideal candidate. I said 'Look, none of this stuff is going to work — everything is changing so fast, just recruit for intelligence — it's the only common factor.'

There was a lot of empty ritual and bull involved in the meetings they had in the old days — so now they don't actually see meetings as a time to make things happen. They say to me afterwards, 'That was a very nice conference. When are we going to do some business?'

In the early days of our Moscow operation — two or three years ago — there were a lot of attempts to get things done by string-pulling, but I gradually showed them that it wouldn't fit with our way of doing business. I think they've accepted that now.

Three-week project: two-and-a-half weeks talking about it, including vodka therapy at the dácha, *then three days of shouting and running about and staying up late — and it gets done. I find it a lot of fun...*

Motivating Russians? Money and foreign travel. Sorry if that's banal, but...

In career development terms, money is not *the only consideration. Having said that, I must add that Russian attitudes to status, knowledge, power and responsibility are very different. You can spend a long time here learning about all that.*

Their education system has emphasised the quantitative. As adults, they're weak in what you might call the soft skills — communication, really. Certainly, they don't anticipate my comfort needs as boss... .

Insist on straight answers. Otherwise, they'll twist the thing around until you've forgotten the question.

Every problem here is an opportunity. The Russians are seriously underestimated; the future is going to be good...We can take all the hassle because this is going to be one hell of a market....

Don't you forget what's divine in the Russian soul — and that's resignation.

Joseph Conrad, *Under Western Eyes*

5

Packing Your Bags

CLOTHES

Be practical

Respect the climate. Most of the Russian land mass lies above the 55th parallel, so the summers are not usually *hot* hot. (Average July highs of 23°C in Moscow.) Dress accordingly — remembering the absence of air conditioning in almost all buildings, and anticipate long, hot, sticky meetings.

The rest of the advice in this section applies to winter.

The winters are *cold* cold. Average lows in December/January of –18°C in Moscow, with Siberia colder still. But if everything is normal, public buildings and apartment blocks are heated to stuffiness (a habit that stems from years of subsidised Soviet energy). Look at the way Russians dress their children for the winter — and the way the *bábushki* will offer strident advice to the parent of any Western child they see in the street who isn't 'properly wrapped up'.

- **Wear numerous layers**, and adjust things as you go.
- **Hat:** On a cold winter's day, a lot of your body heat escapes through the top of your head. Wear a warm hat, or you'll suffer, and the Russians will think you strange.
- **Shoes:** The streets of Russian cities are not the place for patent leather Gucci loafers. Ice, slush, grit, salt, potholes. Wear sensible shoes that will keep out the water and keep in the warmth, and which will allow you to wear an extra pair of socks. Galoshes are useful; all buildings have facilities for shedding unwanted outer garments.

Be polite

- It is considered *nyekultúrny* (impolite, boorish, ignorant) to wear or carry your street clothes into a meeting, and more particularly into a restaurant or theatre. Check your overcoat at the cloakroom and make a proper entrance.

- In private homes, you might be expected to take off your street shoes and slither about in a pair of felt slippers, which stand inside the front door. You help to keep a sheen on the parquet floor.
- In business meetings, taking off your jacket is likely to be seen as a sign of sloppiness or disrespect, rather than a determination to get right down to the nitty-gritty.
- In warm weather, it is considered slobbish (and in women, sluttish) to wear revealing clothes outside the designated areas — poolside or beach. You won't go far wrong if you think of attitudes in the 1950s in Western Europe and the USA.

Be professional

There was a time when the quality of a man's fur hat was an indication of his status — with black sable scoring most points. That was in the days when a fur hat was probably the only item of high quality clothing available to most people outside the tiny élite.

Things have changed now. Yevgenii and his friends are travelling (and shopping) abroad more, and the fur hat has lost its mystique — *but the Russian still has an eye for detail in dress,* and will think the less of you if you do not dress up to your status.

This means he has expectations of you as a Western business person, and you should fulfil them. Fight back the tendency to say 'He'll be wearing a nylon shirt, cellulose suit and plastic shoes, so I'll do the same so as not to upset him.' The smart young business set are spending a lot of money on clothes — and that means the best Italian and French labels. Compete with them if that's how you get your fun.

The less reputable are indulging in flashy ostentation — the crass style that was called in the seventies 'Georgian chic', the style of 'Georgian millionaires' (black market barons). You will see them, and you will not be tempted to emulate them.

For the rest, dress as you would for an important meeting in Munich or Milan.

Note for women

The feminist movement of the 1970s–1980s passed the women of Russia by. Power dressing never happened there. So if you dress in typical Wall Street style, you can expect Russian men — and women — to find you a bit masculine.

On the other hand, if you find yourself working with a Russian woman — banker, engineer, agronomist, whatever — who is enjoying the new range of styles available to her, and dressing in a frankly *feminine* manner, then be careful. Do not categorise her as weak, backward or out of touch. It could be a big mistake.

YOUR SURVIVAL KIT

- **Bath plug:** a favourite piece of advice, dating back to the 1930s. Was there no provision for bath plugs in the Five Year Plan? Did Russians steal them from hotels to repair their cars with? Russians prefer to wash and shave in running water. Will they still do so when they have to pay the full market price for electricity? (In fact a *squash ball* is more useful; it fits any size of plug-hole.)
- **Field rations:** if you are going off the beaten track, travelling by rail, road or air, there will be times when you need comfort and sustenance. The *bufyét* (buffet) will often be closed. Your author always carries a packet of shortbread, some dried apricots, and a quarter-bottle of something warming.
- **Electric adaptor:** 220 volts, 50Hz, 2-pin.
- **Pocket dictionary:** Many transactions can be distilled into a smile and a single word. You just look it up in English and point to the Russian entry.
- **Health and security:** Get insurance, including med-evac. Be sensible with credit cards. Stow a photocopy of passport and visa somewhere.
- **Stationery:** Business cards, with one side in Russian if possible. Some blank letterheads, so you can produce 'A letter from head office'.
- **Cash:** A dollar bill so you can get a luggage cart at the airport. (It's a well-run racket...)

GIFTS

Russians love gifts — giving *and* receiving. Your key business contact, the man who does a bit of fixing for you, the woman steward on the overnight train — there's nothing to lose and everything to gain if you display a bit of generosity.

As students, we traded chewing gum and Western *kitsch* — petrol company give-aways, Beatles key-rings — for *znachki*, the highly collectable enamel badges of Lenin, Kosmos rockets, and power plants.

In the Brezhnev era, no business trip to Russia was a success unless you brought home a kilo or two of coffee-table books (*The Volga, Peoples of the Soviet Union*) and records of Shalyapin's *Boris Godunov* or liturgical chants from Zagorsk.

> *"Most of the Russians I do business with now would be happy to receive a gold Cross pen with their monogram engraved on it."*
>
> Frequent visitor, 1990s

Take good quality knick-knacks with your company logo, city coat of arms, university motto, for people you already know; well-chosen books, videos, magazine subscriptions, well made toys or sweets for their children; 'typically English' (or French, or Italian) goodies to eat or drink; from the airport — little boxes of Belgian chocolates, bottles of posh label drink and perfume.

> *"Offering basic food is still insulting, no matter what the rumours are in the West. Offer little luxuries, with a visibly foreign air."*
>
> *Business Europa*, May/June 1993, Business Brief: Russia

It is not important for your gift to be elaborately wrapped (the opposite of the Japanese tradition); it is the sentiment of giving and receiving which is important.

MUSIC WHILE YOU WORK

Two hundred years ago, the Russian horn band was popular. These *ensembles* were made up of serfs — as many as 40 — playing instruments from half-an-inch to seven feet long. Each musician played only a single note. No contemporary recordings exist, of course. Pity.

The last century gave us the school of amateur composers known as 'The Mighty Handful' — Balakirev, Borodin, Cui, Mussorgsky and Rimsky-Korsakov. They shared the view of the composer Serov:

❝Music...must be inseparable from the people, from its historical development...Russian art can draw inexhaustible forces from the folk element.❞

The folk element is also strong in the works of Tchaikovsky, Russia's first professional composer, who came a little later.

Prokofiev and Stravinsky welcomed the new century with music that was more or less experimental — even startling in its time. Rachmaninov fled the Revolution to live in America.

Under the Soviets, Prokofiev flourished (dying on the same day as Stalin in 1953). Shostakovich and Khachaturyan were the other household names, although Shostakovich had a hard time toeing the party line.

Recommended: Mussorgsky's 'Pictures at an Exhibition' (to make pictures in your mind); Rimsky-Korsakov's 'Sheherazade' (spot the folk tunes); Stravinsky's 'Rite of Spring' (still feels modern 80 years later); Rachmaninov's second symphony (should make you cry); Shostakovich's 'Leningrad Symphony' (composed in 1941 as the Hitlerite armies approached).

PART TWO

The Journey

- A very basic phrasebook to study on the way.
- Ethnographic observations.
- Formalities at the airport — and some reflections on bureaucracy, xenophobia, delays and muddle.
- The drive into town — countryside, buildings old and new, the atmosphere on the streets.
- Extrapolations and discursions on doublethink, graft, and The New Russians.

As we approach our first meeting with Yevgenii Mikhailovich Ivanov, we begin to think about how all these phenomena might appear to him.

6

Useful Expressions

Excuse me! (Can I have your attention?)
Простите! prastítye!

My name is.....
Меня́ зову́т... menyá zavút...

Good morning!/ Good day!/ Good evening!
До́брое у́тро! dóbroye útro! До́брый день! dóbry dyen'!
До́брый ве́чер! dóbry vyécher!

How do you do!/ Pleased to meet you!/ Goodbye!
Здра́вствуйте zdrávstvuitye
Очень прия́тно познако́миться óchen priyátno paznakómit'sya
До свида́ния! do svidániya!

How are you?/ How's it going?
Как вы пожива́ете? kak vy pazhiváyetye?
Как ва́ши дела́ kak váshi dyelá?

Fine/ Very well!/ Not so bad...
Прекра́сно! prikrásno! Хорошо́ kharashó! Норма́льно narmál'na

I would like/ Could I have...please / Thank you!
Мне бы хоте́лось mnye by khatyélas'...
Дайте мне пожа́луйста daite mnye pazhál'sta...
Спаси́бо! spasíba!

Not at all (My pleasure!)
Не́ за что nyé za chto

Excuse me! (I'm sorry!)
Извини́те! izvinítye!

Would you like...?/ May I offer you...?
Не хоте́ли бы вы...? nye khatyéli by vy...?
Позво́льте мне предложи́ть вам... pazvól'tye mnye pridlazhít' vam...

Where is...?
Где? gdye...?

I don't understand.
Я не понима́ю ya nye panimáyu.

Cheers!
На здоро́вье! na zdaróvye

7

Russian Behaviour

FIRST IMPRESSIONS

What might you see in the Russians who share your flight — or serve you? The classic Russian face is Slavic, Finnish and Tatar mixed. Yuri Gagarin. Olga Korbut. Raisa Gorbachev.

Russian Behaviour

Russians in a group do not exude easy *bonhomie*. To some Russians, the 'keep smiling' behaviour of Westerners (and particularly Americans) appears naive and insipid.

Whether or not there is a racial predisposition to pessimism, the history to date of the Russian *naród* (people/ race/ nation) is one of endurance rather than easy success.

> *"...their staying power, their essential stability amidst the turbulent currents of violent change, chaotic upheaval, and sudden innovation..."*
>
> Tibor Szamuely, *The Russian Tradition*

When things are going right, and the Russian smile does come, it is open and sincere.

Russians don't wave their arms around when they talk; it is all quite contained. They avoid pointing fingers at each other, which would be rude.

Nor are their faces very mobile. Perhaps this is a combination of Asian inscrutability and a wish to avoid what Ronald Hingley describes as *facecrime* — 'failure to simulate adequate political subservience'.

Sign language from the old days

He's a KGB man: two fingers on the shoulder (military stripes).

This conversation is bugged: point up at imaginary chandelier.

Brezhnev: curved index fingers as eyebrows.

On the other hand, they have smaller buffer zones than, say, Swedes. They get into each other's space, put their faces close together to talk, place reassuring hands on one another's forearms. They jostle and shove each other to get through turnstiles or up gangplanks — without hard feelings.

When you pass as a stranger and look at a Russian, he does not stare back (as an Italian might). On the other hand, during a conversation, eye contact is steady and level between the participants (unlike the Chinese habit).

When Russians sit, they hold themselves upright; they don't sprawl, lounge or slump. When they are engaged in a conversation, they give it their full attention. Taking a walk with a keen Russian conversationalist can be a slow business; he will demand frequent halts while he makes his points.

8

Immigration

Immigration officers all over the world lack obvious charm. The Russian ones are no exception.

BUREAUCRACY

Ever since Lenin, bureaucracy has been anathema; the 'satirical' magazine *Krokodil* carried anti-bureaucratic diatribes and cartoons even in the 1960s.

> Time for a clear-out! Get rid of all these files! But first, make a copy of each, just to be on the safe side...

The Soviets failed to eradicate bureaucracy, because the roots are deep and strong and gnarled.

Custine again, in 1839:

> *"The profusion of small, superfluous precautions creates here a population of clerks. Each one of these men discharges his duty with a pedantry, a rigor, an air of importance uniquely designed to give prominence to the most obscure employment."*

XENOPHOBIA

There is a long tradition in Russia of mistrust of the foreigner, and Custine complained about that, too.

General Walter Bedell Smith was American Ambassador in Moscow in the late 1940s and he read Custine's *Journey for Our Time*.

> *"My own position and that of my staff as foreign diplomats in the Soviet Union showed little variation from that of our*

predecessors accredited to the Czarist court a century before. In both eras one finds the same restrictions, the same surveillance, the same suspicion."

The immigration official who is giving you a cold stare is a border guard; he has been trained to see his job as protecting his country.

DELAYS

Things might take a little time at immigration. This gives you time to adjust your body clock to a different tempo.

Ferdinand Protzman was a German banker in Russia in 1989:

"*Many American businessmen come to Moscow and leave three weeks later completely frustrated. German businessmen are willing to stay six months to make a deal.*"

New York Times, 15 June 1989

MUDDLE

Dogged they might be, but Germans are also known for their love of *ordnung* — order. They must often clench their teeth at the Russian propensity for *besporyádok* — disorder.

Things are improving all the time, of course, but Russian airports still have some way to go before they can compare with Munich or Cologne.

The Russians, in turn, laugh behind their hands at each fresh expression of German *punctilio*. This is the source of much of the humour in the novel *Oblomov*, by Goncharov (written 1849–59). Stolz, a half-German, fails entirely to bring order to the life of Oblomov, a feckless, slovenly dreamer who spends the first fifty pages trying to get out of bed.

On your first visit, it is a good thing if you can arrange for someone to meet you, and help you get on your way into town. Airport taxi ranks are a magnet for scoundrels the world over.

9

View from your Car Seat

Ribbon development along the road from airport to city, perhaps, but behind that you should see glimpses of field and forest.

THE COUNTRYSIDE

Russian nationalism is steeped in the mystical idea of *ródina* — motherland, from *rod*, meaning family, stock, genus, generation. Not surprisingly, Russians feel closest to *ródina* when they are tending the strawberries and potatoes in the garden of their *dacha*, hunting mushrooms in the woods (a national passion), pursuing game with rod and gun (and virtual wilderness is never very far away).

Turgenev's collection of atmospheric short stories, *A Huntsman's Sketches* (1847–52), perfectly captures the allure of the Russian countryside, while treating the peasantry in an innovative way — as human beings endowed with thoughts and feelings (it was the eve of emancipation).

As you enter the city, be alert for churches and monastic buildings, palaces and fortresses.

THE ANCIENT

The ecclesiastical architectural forms have grown around the 'inscribed cross' floor plan: a cuboid centre piece with dome, at the crossing point of two wide aisles. Often there is a proliferation of cupolas above that. Built of brick, stone or wood — some of the latter still standing since the 16th century.

The palaces, theatres and museums, beginning with Peter the Great's new capital, are a parade of imported styles, commissioned from imported architects — Swedes and Dutch for northern European baroque, French and Italian for Neo-classicism — buildings and parks — in the time of Catherine. It was all designed to impress. Custine on St Petersburg:

"I cannot believe myself out-of-doors when I see so many pompous, delicate, brilliant things...I cannot keep from being filled with admiration."

Moscow meanwhile remained the *bol'sháya derévnya — the big village*, although the centre of the city was developed, using Russian architects, by the nobility and wealthy merchants — Neo-classical shading into pseudo-Gothic.

There was a 'Russian revival' in the late 19th century, drawing on old Muscovite decorative elements, folk-art and motifs from wooden architecture.

'The Kremlin' is not just the group of buildings in the centre of Moscow. *Kreml'* means fortress, and many towns have them. Given the importance of waterways in Russia's early development, kremlins are often sited above strategic bends and confluences of rivers.

The ancient buildings of Russia were immaculately preserved by the Bolsheviks, and restored when damaged in war — an expression of national pride in cultural heritage.

THE SOVIET

Examples of *Art Nouveau* and *Art Deco* can be found, and the years after the Revolution saw a brief flowering of the *avant-garde* — including opportunities for experiments in Constructivism (railway stations, workers' clubs, factories).

From 1932, all this was squashed by the single Union of Soviet Architects. Socialist Realism, and the Stalinist 'wedding cake' style — ministries, museums, hotels — started to dominate the squares, and the skyline.

After the war, reconstruction was urgent and money was short. The suburbs of the cities are sprawls of gimcrack, soulless, repetitive apartment blocks, where people somehow get along in their allocated living spaces — four square metres each in the 1950s buildings, when the agreed 'healthy minimum' was nine.

Things got better in the 1970s, as large-panel construction systems were developed, and 'walls' of apartments sprang up at the published rate of one dwelling per minute. These were generally thought to be more liveable-in.

The architecture of the Soviet period fitted the *zeitgeist* :

> *"The ideas in modern Russia are machine-cut blocks coming in solid colours; the nuance is outlawed, the interval walled up, the curve grossly stepped."*
>
> Vladimir Nabokov, *Pale Fire* (1962)

It was not vindictiveness or anti-bourgeois bigotry that led Soviet planners to build this way.

> *"Lenin and his government ... found themselves committed to establishing a heaven on earth in a territory which...had become a fairly near approximation to hell. Such were the devastations, human and material, inflicted by seven years of war, first against Germany and then against the forces of White Russia. No power on earth could have restored so shattered a realm for many years or even decades, and it was therefore necessary to mobilise the weapon of pretence...the whole of...the USSR was converted into a giant simulated prestige project."*
>
> Ronald Hingley, *The Russian Mind*

Orwell coined the terms *doublethink* and *newspeak* in 1948, to describe the thought processes and language of totalitarian propaganda. The Russian varieties have a longer history.

Economical with the truth

In the early seventies, your author was with a group of British and American students on a Russian language course in Sochi, on the Black Sea coast. We were offered a good price on a day's excursion by air to Tbilisi, the Georgian capital, and about twenty of us signed up for the trip.

We took off on time, flew South East between the sea and the Caucasus mountains, arrived over Tbilisi *in bright sunshine*, circled the airport twice, and returned to Sochi.

A landing had been impossible, we were told, because 'The weather is bad in Tbilisi'. This became a catchphrase for the group, used as an incantation when things went badly and the explanations were feeble.

This happened against the background of a subdued cholera scare. The World Health Organisation had issued warnings about outbreaks thousands of kilometres away in Pakistan, and the Russian authorities had closed the Sochi area off to road traffic.

Russian friends — the disaffected, naughty type we met on the beach — wrote this off as a *gosudárstvennaya shútka* (government joke). The real reason they had closed the roads, they said, was to make it impossible for the tramps of Russia to migrate to Sochi, where the previous year a great shanty town had been built on the beach, to the embarrassment of the authorities (Sochi being the Pearl of the Black Sea Coast.) We didn't know whether to believe this when we heard it. Was Slava spinning a yarn?

We checked with other friends — the pious, well-behaved kind we met at language class. Slava must be wrong, they said, because 'There are no tramps in Russia'. Nor, according to these people, were there any black marketeers or prostitutes.

We knew the black marketeers well, and had sold them our Wrangler jeans and Polaroid sunglasses; we watched the prostitutes — 'taxi girls' — from the hotel balcony in the evening, working the promenade and the park. So maybe there were tramps as well. But was there ever a shanty town? And what about the cholera anyway? Had it perhaps reached Tbilisi? Should we tell the World Health Organisation? Or should we just buy a watermelon, scoop the middle out, fill it up with ice and vodka, scrounge some drinking straws, and have a party?

A FAMILY OF WORDS

Every language has many words for shades of dishonesty, and Russian is no exception.

Vranyó

If Slava *was* making the whole thing up about the shanty town, he was indulging in *vranyó* — fibs, non-vindictive lying, blarney, persiflage, leg-pulling, bullshit, talking it up.

(*lozh* — deliberate manipulative lying, is a different thing entirely. *Ty vryosh!* is OK — 'you're kidding!', but *ty lzhosh* — 'you're a liar!' is very harsh.)

Pre-revolutionary Vranyó

In 'Revizor' (*The Government Inspector*, 1836), Gogol' gives us a timeless exposé of corruption and fear in a provincial town. The local worthies are taken for a ride by Khlyestakov, a drifter whom they mistake for a government official on a sneak inspection. They treat him royally, bribe him shamelessly, and throw the mayor's wife and daughter at him. The key to the comedy is that Khlyestakov has not actually set out to cheat them; he just gets carried away on a tide of *vranyó*, and feeds them the inflated nonsense they want to hear — that he is the Tsar's most trusted adviser, that he has a personal staff of hundreds, that he can do them all kinds of favours back in the capital.

Russians in the theatre audience are gripped by the artistry of Khlyestakov's performance; *vranyó* is folk art. (The Danny Kaye movie didn't quite catch it.)

> *"Half-way through a story, you generally begin to believe it yourself...yet when you go to bed at night...you suddenly say, 'O God, what a lot of rubbish I was talking!'"* .
>
> Dostoevsky, 'One or two words about vranyó', in *Diary of a Writer*

Dostoevsky himself created a classic *vranyó* addict in General Ivolgin (who appears in *The Idiot*, 1869). Ivolgin, with no hope of being believed, tells the hero, Prince Myshkin, that he was once Napoleon's page and had himself persuaded the great man to retreat from Moscow. To honour his end of the unspoken *vranyó* contract, Myshkin keeps a straight face throughout.

Every Russian recognises displays of *vranyó*, many admire it when it is well done, and some admit to getting a special buzz from perpetrating it.

> *"Just before you're found out, you do seem to come to life for a moment."*
>
> Leonid Andreyev, *Pan-Russian Vranyó*

Soviet Vranyó

The Soviet brand of communism harnessed the tradition of *vranyó*, as it harnessed so many others. Yevgenii's generation grew up under Khrushchev, the Peasant Premier, who was less committed than Lenin, less scheming than Stalin, and certainly more ebullient than Brezhnev. He was given to flights of *braggadocio*, and made of it a weapon in his statesmanship — a slippery and unpredictable opponent.

So when Yevgenii thinks of *vranyó*, he is likely to bracket it with *tuftá*.

Tuftá

Tuftá was institutionalised Soviet bullshit. The word covers the range from an Intourist guide telling the baffled tour group that the shabby block of flats is a workers' paradise, to inflated grain harvests, to Stalin-era claims that everything from the telephone to the game of baseball was invented first by a Russian.

Russians of Yevgenii's generation, exposed to a lifetime of *tuftá* and inured to it, are often sceptical when their Western business partners show them business plans, sales projections or presentations about corporate vision-and-value. *Take all that with a pinch of salt, can't we?*

Tufta in its turn overlaps with *pokazukha*.

Pokazúkha

Pokazúkha is the show-off stuff — close to *ochkovtirátelstvo* (eyewash) — and it goes back most famously to the eighteenth century, when Potemkin, a favourite in Catherine the Great's court, made sure that the excursions of the tsarina into the countryside always found the routes lined with the latest thing in rural housing, and happy, healthy peasants. Paper-thin pretence, of course, but who was about to tell her that?

So when visiting Western delegations were shown only the working part of a dam, and fudged-up statistics on its performance, that was the 'Potemkin village' syndrome — *pokazukha*. Socialist realist art — Merry Peasants at the Collective Farm Banquet Drink a Health to the Father of His People — is an expression of the same drive. The same attitude made Khrushchev personally furious with Pasternak for publishing *Doctor Zhivago* abroad — he was washing the state's dirty linen in public.

You find *pokazukha* all over the world, of course. Some Americans said the moon landings were a sham, and I have heard the head of an American pharmaceuticals company brag over breakfast to his subordinates how, in his younger days, he faked a complete production line to impress the State Governor when he came on a visit. (The Five-Year Plan, after all, is not so very different from the ambitious Project Plan in a big corporation.)

It is not surprising that some Russians, on official trips West in the seventies, admired the first big supermarket they visited — not as an example of how the free market can work, but for the skill and thoroughness with which the Potemkin Village had been built. They just *knew* it couldn't be real.

As with *vranyó*, there is a two-way process here: the recipient has to play ball with the performer. It wrecks the whole game if you say, 'I can't believe Napoleon would take advice from his page', or 'Could you switch it off and on again, so I can see if it works a second time?'

How our Yevgenii sees it

For Yevgenii Mikhailovich's generation, *tufta* and *pokazukha* just had to be lived with.

In the Soviet period, where we outsiders might merely think of propaganda, he was being trained in an interconnected system of half-truths.

When he looked up and saw the advertisements for the state: 'The Ideas of Lenin Live and Conquer', 'The Communist Party is the Glory of the Motherland', his face went blank and he processed the messages according to the rules of the game. Just like when we see a dubious slogan for soap powder.

Yevgenii still awaits proof that he and his family really can have a better life in the free market. Until he has that proof, he will reserve judgement on the promises of Western governments, institutes and corporations.

WHAT'S NEW ON THE STREET?

Statues and slogans

The slogans of Marxism-Leninism are coming down off the rooftops, and the demolition of Stalin statues has provided the world's press with many photo-opportunities. (Where such slogans and statues remain, you will know yourself to be in the 'Red Belt' — where support for reforms is weak.)

Going back up: statues of Alexander III, the tsar who instituted the 1890s attempt to capitalise and industrialise the country; Marshal Zhukhov, victor of Stalingrad, who was swept under the carpet so the Party could take all the credit.

The new billboards, of course, advertise banks, up-market cars, cosmetics, business magazines.

Bricks and mortar

Or rather steel, concrete and glass. Real estate values have skyrocketed; commercial space is dearer than in Tokyo. Some Western companies (like McDonald's) have found the answer to problems repatriating rouble profits: use the roubles to build a shiny new office block downtown, rent it out at a profit, re-invest that profit in further property...

Hustle and bustle

Lining up the financing on a property deal is tricky, like almost any other piece of substantial business. Lots of buzzy little meetings in hotel lobbies, and on street corners.

A few key words will give you an idea of how things happened under the centrally planned economy (which was incapable of fruitful activity within the rules):

BLAT	Graft; pull; what the French call 'piston'
SVYÁZI	Links; connections; strings to pull
KOMBINÁTSIYA	The exercise of blat and svyazi
VZYÁTKA	Kickback; bribe
TOLKÁCH	Pusher — meaning fixer; negotiator; red tape cutter
ZASHCHÍTNIK	Defender — an official who keeps other officials off your back

Some of the people scurrying along the pavements in the business district are still about this kind of work.

> “*When* blat *dies there will be no funeral. How will we get hold of a coffin and nails?*”

Is that unique to Russia?

Corruption and crime

An extension of the above.

> *“‘Mafia’ had been a part of the Russian political vocabulary for more than twenty years, covering such a variety of sins in Soviet life as to be almost undefinable.”*
>
> Stephen Handelman, *Comrade Criminal*

You probably won’t see any criminal activity from your airport limo, but your imagination will be working overtime, fuelled by reports in the Western press. The authorities are working on it, well aware that serious foreign investment is being discouraged by the unscrupulous and vicious.

The *Economist* of 9 July 1994 carried figures showing a decline in the previous twelve months in murder, rape, aggravated assault, robbery, embezzlement — with bribery up slightly. (Russian statistics are rarely the very best, and in an area like *bribery*, who can really say?)

The article goes on to describe the mergers taking place among Russia’s estimated 5800 gangs (those figures again), and to break down ‘mafia’ operations into four categories. At one end of the scale is the small businessman who sells dodgy goods from a kiosk, whose prices are high because he pays protection money, at the other, the neanderthals in track suits and gold chains, in their hot BMWs, who also run girls, drugs and arms, thus providing a service to the ‘businessmen’... ‘whose methods hover somewhere between those of Al Capone and the early American robber-barons. Usually these big-timers made their first few million by bribing the fourth and most deadly of the species: the state mafia

...Types one and three (the small- and big-time “businessmen”) need to be encouraged to go legitimate. Types two and four (the hoods and corrupt officials) need stamping out.’

If it takes authoritarian measures to achieve this end, says Aleksei Izyumov, then so be it.

> *“Of the two evils — crime and authoritarianism — Russia should choose the lesser one.”*
>
> *Newsweek*, 29 August 1994

Rich and poor

Much of the crime at street level is fuelled by unemployment. The most dismal parts of Russian cities are around the main rail termini, where the hopeless and the marginalised cluster.

The world's newspapers have carried photo-montages of the poor and the New Rich. The latter you will observe in the lobbies, bars and 'malls' of the expensive new hotels, and the night clubs.

As long ago as the 1970s, there was talk of a 'gilded youth' — the children of the well-placed *nomenklatúra*. Much the same people have now discovered the pleasures of conspicuous consumption. Or is it so pleasurable? Leonid Zhukhovitsky visited a night club and admired the pretty girls on the dancefloor.

> "*On the other hand, it was infuriating to note how bored these men in their bright jackets were. Surely they did not pay an entrance fee of R60,000 for nothing. And if they came to pick up a girl, why didn't they do just that? Instead, they just sat and drank...*
>
> *The children they are now sending off to posh finishing schools and colleges will one day be embarrassed by the vulgarity of their parents.*"
>
> *Delovie Lyudi*, December 1994

Buying and selling

Whatever their children's future, for the moment the *nouveaux riches* have plenty of *báksi* and *gríni* (bucks/ greenbacks) to spend on the fine Western products in the shops.

One of the most poignant sights in Moscow is the lower floor of *Détskiy Mir* (Children's World), the old showpiece toyshop — now given over to a showroom stocked with sporty four-wheel drive toys for grown-ups.

At the other end of the spectrum are the *lárki* (kiosks) — (16,000 in Moscow at the last count). David Remnick recorded:

> "...a lace tablecloth, a bottle of Curaçao, Wrigley's spearmint gum, Mars bars, a Public Enemy tape, Swiss chocolate, plastic 'marital toys', a Mercedes-Benz hood ornament, American cigarettes, and Estonian pornography."

Somewhere in between, Nik's 24-hour American supermarket: *Cap'n Crunch, Del Monte, Smuckers...Planters, Ruffles, Ragu...Betty Crocker ...Ocean Spray, Rubber Maid, Hershey's, Mrs Butterworth, Bisquick, Red Baron...*; and the Manhattan-Express restaurant: *Gin and Lemon braised French Goose, Oven Roasted Pheasant with Cranberry and thyme relish...Saturday is 'live lobster day'...*

But the market (*rýnok*) for luxury items is flattening out — at least until the economy in general begins to heal a bit faster.

> *"For the first few years it's been easy for my customers. They load up at my depot, truck the stuff to their warehouse, sprinkle a few advertisements about — 'I've got this to sell, I've got that to sell' — and wait for the phone to ring. Things are tightening up now — it's reaching saturation point. They'll have to get pro-active if they want to survive the next round..."*
>
> Importer of branded liquor

Cut and thrust

Look up from your airport limo, and you might spot a TV satellite dish. It is debatable which has more influence — CNN or MTV. Home-grown Russian TV has changed out of recognition, and the politicians are learning to manipulate its power, and face aggressive interviews.

Below on the pavement, posters and fliers for parties, lobbies, and cults.

Optimists speak of democratisation. Pessimists favour the word *bespredel'* — without limits. The determinists are waiting for the pendulum to swing back, and for strict limits to be set once again — a new period of authoritarianism. This is what underlies the fears of fascism.

How our Yevgenii sees it

What does Yevgenii Mikhailovich make of all this change? It depends very much on how he and his loved ones are doing out of it. And, as we said in the Introduction, our Yevgenii is a survivor...

PART THREE

The First 24 Hours

- Comfort and survival tips
- First contact with your Russian business partners (including Yevgenii Mikhailovich) — and how to handle introductions and small talk.
- A few more notes on the Russian language: social register; the new language of business; and areas of confusion between English and Russian.

10

Survival and Comfort

The Russia Survival Guide, Where in Moscow and *Where in St Petersburg*, all by Paul E. Richardson, are very good. This book does not aim to be so comprehensive.

Just a few thoughts...

HOTEL

- **Joint-venture Hotels** — Westernised, pricey, motivated staff, good service.
- **Russian-owned/ State-owned Hotels** — none of the above. (One compensation is the renowned *dezhurnaya* — the woman porter/ concierge/ holder of the keys who inhabits each floor. Part of the challenge of a stay in such a hotel is to get on the right side of her. Chocolates and baby photos?)

If travelling to a town you don't know, ask your host to arrange/ recommend decent accommodation for you.

EATING OUT

Similar to the hotel market, plus a lot of pizzeria/ burger/ ice cream outlets, Japanese/ French/ Italian restaurants, and a new wave of high class, classic Russian cuisine at serious prices.

For medium-price spicy, London has Indian, Paris has Vietnamese, Amsterdam has Indonesian. Moscow has Georgian.

(A recent survey showed that one per cent of Muscovites take dinner in a restaurant of any description in a given year,)

In Russian restaurants, the *zakúski* — hors d'oeuvres are an important stage, and might make up a sizeable part of the bill. They might be thrust upon you, unless you stipulate *chístiy stol* — a clear table. *Salad* often means some combination of potato, beetroot, onion, maize, and chicken pieces bound in mayonnaise. *Shampánskoye* — *méthode champenoise* — tends to be sweet.

Big Russian restaurants traditionally cater for groups, not individuals. If you dine alone the waiters might find it hard to remember you are there.

If you are being entertained by a Russian host, and you think he might get stuck paying out of his own pocket, offer to pay half at least. Expense account living is not fully developed, and that bill could be a month's wages for him. On the other hand, don't be too ostentatious. Tip 10–15 per cent.

CURRENCY

You can do a lot these days with credit cards. Beware special in-house exchange rates, especially in the bars of trendy hotels. If buying more than a pocketful of roubles, shop around for a good rate and take local advice. Stay legal.

TRANSPORT

- Be wary of pirate **taxis** — especially in areas where you would seek victims if *you* were a bit of a villain. Otherwise, the *chástnik* — moonlighting amateur — is a valuable addition to the city's infrastructure, since you can flag one down on any street. Negotiate price in advance. If you want a smart, official car and a receipt, your hotel will fix you up. Some drivers take it as an insult if you sit in the back seat.
- Moscow's **Metro** is one of the great sights — elegant, clean and efficient. There are **buses** of various kinds, once you begin to get a feel for the city's layout. Get local advice on how to buy tickets.
- Longer distance, **trains** these days might be safer and more reliable than **planes**. This situation will change again as Western and western-style airlines (like *Transaero*) increase their penetration of the hinterland.
- **Driving** takes a bit of getting used to. The *GAI* (traffic police) will let you know — and quite likely fine you — if you make an illegal turn (easily done) or drive a dirty car (sometimes difficult to avoid).

SHOPPING

Westernised boutiques and supermarkets will feel perfectly familiar to you. Traditional Soviet-era shops still operate the *queue-to-choose-your-goods, queue-to-pay-and-get-a-ticket, queue-to-present-your-ticket-and-pick-up-your-goods* system. (Some analysts believe that this arrangement was a cause of shortages. People faced with this palaver would buy more than they really wanted, and hoard the goods they bought.)

TELECOMMUNICATIONS

Improving all the time, in concentric rings spreading from key commercial centres. One aspect of the infrastructure that has been attracting foreign investment. *E-mail* is the big growth story.

Even Soviet-era hotels now realise they won't get many Western business guests unless they offer at least a decent telephone and fax service.

PERSONAL SECURITY

Don't tempt fate with large wads of cash, expensive cameras, or solo excursions into rough areas after dark.

11

First Contact

Having unpacked, got your bearings, eaten, and slept off the time difference, you are ready for your first business meeting.

SETTING IT UP

We hope you haven't come this far without a few appointments and introductions. Otherwise, you might find that office-holders are often unavailable and secretaries loath to pass on messages (keep your temper!). For this reason, players of the system treasure the number of the telephone which rings directly on the desk of the mover-and-shaker.

To get an idea of *their* background and style of operation, you should meet on *their* territory some time, but it might be convenient to have the first meeting in your hotel.

Don't be ambitious with the agenda for the first meeting; in other words, allow plenty of time for exploration, ceremonial pleasantries, and ritual sniffing.

Try to get full versions of their names and titles in advance, so you can start learning them.

THE NAME GAME

The exchange of business cards is quite formal. Pay proper respect to the cards you are given, and take the opportunity to check the pronunciation — especially the syllable-stress — of the name. *'Please, am I saying this correctly: Dobrolyúbov?'*

Titles, patronymics, and introducing yourself

Továrishch ('comrade') is gone forever, along with *grazhdán'ka* ('female citizen') — unless you are mixing with traditional communists who are making a point.

The traditional *góspodin* and *gospózha* are now used in formal situations. Your hotel clerk will address guests as 'Mr Pickwick', 'Madame Bovary', 'Gospodin Karamazov' or 'Gospozha Karenina'. But for you to use this form in business or social life would seem cold and stiff.

The traveller to Ireland might be surprised at how quickly strangers use his first name; Germans can stay on *Herr Schmidt/Herr Müller* terms for life.

The trick in Russia is to master the name-plus-patronymic system, and then discipline yourself to use it.

In literature

If you have ever tackled a big Russian novel, you will have seen the list of characters at the beginning.

The coachman will probably be listed as *Fedya* or some such — the affectionate/familiar form of *Fedor*.

If the local doctor appears, he is down as *Dr Popov*, unless he is a real part of the action or a friend of the main characters.

In that case, we are given his full name:

SERGEI	ALEXANDROVICH	POPOV
First name	father's first name	family name
	('PATRONYMIC')	
ímya.........................	ótchestvo...............................	famíliya

In a man's full name, the patronymic is his father's first name with an ending tacked on — *...ovich* or *...evich*, usually. A woman also inherits her father's name, but with a feminine ending — *...ovna* or *...evna* being common.

In business

When you, our traveller, first meet Yevgenii, you should address him as

Yevgenii Mikhailovich

As with the Americans (and unlike the more reserved English), Russians pepper their conversation with quite frequent repetitions of the name. To show a combination of warmth and respect, they use

FIRST NAME PLUS PATRONYMIC

***Skazhíte, Boris Sergeevich* — Tell me, Boris Sergeevich...**

Family and friends

Tatyana is *Tanya* or *Tanyushka* ('diminutive forms') to her friends, and the boys ask *Sasha* (Alexander) out to play football.

If your working relationship with Yevgenii becomes friendship, you might make the step to first-name-only. When he seems to be comfortable calling you plain 'John' or 'Peter', you can do the same with him.

At a later stage (in the *bánya*? When you get drunk together?), he might invite you to address him as *Zhénya*, or *Zhénichka*.

(At about the same time, you can switch from *vy* to *ty*. You surely know of other examples: *vous* to *tu*, or *sie* to *du*. English lost the option when it dropped *thou*.)

Study these examples from Turgenev's *Fathers and Sons*:

Young Arkady brings a friend home from university. 'Papa...let me introduce my great friend Bazarov, whom I have so often mentioned in my letters...' (Arkady addresses Bazarov simply as Yevgeny throughout.)

Old Nikolai Petrovich shakes Bazarov's hand: 'I am indeed glad...But might I inquire your name?' 'Yevgenii Vassilyich', Bazarov replied in a lazy but virile voice... 'I hope, my dear Yevgenii Vassilyich, you won't find it dull with us...'

Bazarov rapidly demonstrates that he is a man of the people: 'Hurry up, old bushy-beard!', said Bazarov, addressing the driver.

'Did you hear that, Mitya?' chipped in the driver's mate....

Bazarov does find country life dull, and seeks to divert himself with Anna Sergeyevna Odintsova, widow of old Odintsov, born Anna Sergeyevna Lokteva, daughter of Sergei Nikolayevich Loktev. She keeps him at arm's length, and they stay on first-name-plus-patronymic terms.

(If that makes the book sound banal, I apologise. It has masses of social history, and a duel, and an elegant structure. Turgenev was 'the novelist's novelist'.)

Back to business

The memory of a Russian is trained from childhood to deal with all this. Many internationalised Russians recognise that foreigners have faulty memories, and try to help by simplifying things for you.

Young Russians meeting American students on Black Sea beaches would sometimes introduce themselves as 'Harry', or 'Jim' — using the English names they had been given at secondary school for use during their English classes.

A secretary or a young manager in a joint venture might permit Western associates to use diminutives — *Katya* or *Tolya.*

Yevgenii considers this casual approach to be a bit un-Russian — a flashy Moscow/St Petersburg practice. With him and his colleagues, it is worth the extra mental effort to follow the more traditional rules.

Introducing yourself

It is always difficult to grasp a foreign name the first time it is thrown at us. Your Russian counterpart would like to get your name first time. His chances are much improved if you emulate 007: 'My name is Bond, *James* Bond.'

This method gives the vital surname twice, and the emphasis suggests that you are prepared to be addressed by your first name.

HOSPITALITY

As a business visitor, you will encounter old-style Russian hospitality, which is sincere and generous, and more 'sophisticated' styles of entertainment, which are not noticeably Russian at all.

Very Russian is the conference table spread with sweets, cakes and mineral water, as well as the usual tea and coffee. Cups of tea, rather awkwardly, are filled to the very brim, so as not to appear grudging.

Working lunches don't get much work done — and skip lunch if you've been invited out to dinner later.

"There are two kinds of expatriate here. The ones who go jogging, and spend the rest of their free time looking for a good salad bar, and the ones who give up, and live on meat and dumplings. Care for another dumpling?"

Briton in Russia

"I was astonished the first time I had dinner in an English home. Chelsea. First course — one slice of smoked salmon...cut so thin I could see the pattern on the plate."

Russian in England

GOOD MANNERS

Homo sovieticus was not famous for his *savoir-faire*. Western journalists have had a lot of fun penetrating the etiquette schools which have sprung up in Moscow to help the New Russians re-learn the arts of dress sense, table talk, and canapé-balancing.

On the other hand, the general social code in Russia has always been quite conservative — even prim. Hands in pockets? Chewing gum? Feet on the train seat opposite? Whistling in the street? *Nyekultúrny!*

Shake hands formally on meeting. Practise your bear-hug/ kissing technique by all means, but let your Russian host make the first move.

Don't display nervous impatience. If things are going too slowly, indicate clearly that you are ready to move on, and then be calm.

Respect the formality that obtains between different members of their delegation. If you establish cordial relations, and get on nickname-terms with one of the senior Russians, be careful not to use the diminutive form when speaking of him to his junior colleagues.

CORDIAL RELATIONS

Two things should be happening in parallel at your first meeting — sizing up the business prospects, and working out how you are going to connect as people.

A Russian will call on his friend in the middle of the night without warning, and walk straight to the refrigerator to see if there's anything good to eat. If you can get something of that atmosphere in your business dealings, then you're doing well. (If head office back in New

York or Düsseldorf say they are more interested in the bottom line, tell them this *is* the bottom line.)

Your author ran a one-day seminar for a mixed group of Central and East Europeans on Lake Balaton, in Hungary. It culminated in a good dinner, after which it was one of the Russians who said, 'I imagine you picked up a bottle of something good at Heathrow?'. I went to my room to get the litre of malt, and handed it over. He pulled out the cork and threw it away. He was telling me he liked me.

Russians can be refreshingly direct — or intrusive, depending on your perception. Dr Robert Lyall lived in Russia in the early 19th century:

> *"With as much ease as they say 'How do you do?', they ask the most impertinent questions, with respect to your connections and family, your property and revenues, and your secret affairs and private opinions. An evasive answer only prompts their curiosity."*

In return, they are open with information about themselves. *Kak dyelá?* — How are things? — will often earn more than a simple *Normál'no.*

> *"Why should I say 'I am fine' when I feel bad after illness? Russians are more straightforward."*
>
> Russian woman living in London

Between themselves, Russians are quite open about material matters — *Where did you buy it? How much did it cost? How's the new job? How much are they paying you?* Given the painful disparity between Russian and Western income levels, it is best not to initiate such a conversation. But if a Russian starts it, don't prevaricate.

Artificiality, shallowness, pretentiousness — these the Russian detests, preferring *umiléniye* — tenderness, openness, the free expression of sentiment.

SUPERSTITIONS

- If giving flowers, give an odd number. Even numbers are for funerals.

- Don't shake hands over the threshold. Step right inside/ outside for the greeting.
- When setting out on a journey, sit for a while and reflect — and give your soul time to settle back in your body. (It might have wandered off somewhere... .)

12

Language – Further Observations

As you meet Yevgenii Mikhailovich and his colleagues for the first time, the linguistic idea of *register* comes into play. Register is where language meets social nuance; we speak in a *formal register* when we are introduced to the Queen, and adopt a *matey register* with an Australian in the pub.

When business is being discussed, traditional Russian vocabulary is a bit inadequate. After all, for 70 years nobody was speaking of profit margins, let alone discounted cash flow forecasting, unique selling propositions, and business process re-engineering. There are many *neologisms* and *loan words*.

On your side, when you are speaking English, perhaps through a long-suffering interpreter, there are certain rules you should observe in the interests of *being clear*.

REGISTER

From the time of Peter the Great, Russian was considered a crude instrument. Until Pushkin's time, French was the language of the court; it was Pushkin (early 19th century) who gave the Russian language its rich and varied literary voice. (Parallels with Shakespeare.)

In *The Bronze Horseman*, Pushkin uses ponderous phrasing and orotund vocabulary to describe Peter the Great and his vision. He switches to short, chopped everyday language for the passages about the humble clerk.

"...there are two distinct Russian languages: the low-style, demotic tongue, based ultimately on peasant usage, in which ordinary events such as the loss of a collar-stud or the price of a

bottle of vodka may be discussed; and the priestly or hieratic argot, deriving partly from Church Slavonic, in which such matters as the notional fulfilment of notional norms, the 'achievements' of 'workers' and other liturgical or 'musical' material is traditionally couched."

Ronald Hingley, *The Russian Mind*

(In the diverse registers of modern English, something similar happens with Anglo-Saxon — for everyday needs, and Latin — for conceptual discussion.)

The choice between *vy* — you and *ty* — thou is a question of register. In a traditional Russian organisation, *ty* was very sparingly used. A Swede working in Moscow:

"*The CEO came over from Göteborg on a state visit. Some of my Russians understand Swedish — and they were very surprised at how freely Mr Big was using the familiar form of address. Of course, it was his usual way of making things jolly and informal, but on this occasion it made things just a bit uncomfortable...*"

A note on swearing, the *uncouth* register, in Russian called *mat*: Russian is a fine language for swearing in, combining blasphemy, gynaecological obscenity, racism and toilet-talk, and with a touch of contortionism thrown in. When a Russian swears at you, he tells you things about your mother and sister, and suggests you perform acts with yourself that most of us couldn't manage.

NEOLOGISMS AND LOAN-WORDS

Russian creates many good words in combination with a Latin stem. A helicopter is a *vertolyót* — literally 'vertical flyer'.

More generally, whenever the Russian historical pendulum swung in the direction of *liberalisation*, the language sucked in a rush of new words, to express the new ideas that came from outside.

Sometimes the foreign word was broken down into its Latin components, and translated stem-by-stem into Russian. So *in-de-pend-ence* = not-from-hanging-ness = *ne-za-vísi-most'*, and *hydrogen* = water-born = *vodo-ród*.

Sometimes the foreign term is brought in complete — *bás-gitárist*, and sometimes with Russian endings tagged on: *fizícheskaya khímiya* from 'physical chemistry'.

In the new Business Russia, the business journalists are teaching themselves to write in a catchy, knowing, Westernised style. Among themselves they might use a lot of home-grown *zhargon: kapústa* = cabbage = money; *shíshka* = lump/growth/excrescence = boss.

More mundanely, words like *ménedzhment, infrastruktúra, marketing* and *brand* have been adopted. Some Russians work hard to find Russian language equivalents, others cheerfully use the American words.

BEING CLEAR

Many middle-aged Russians you will meet speak elegant, rapid English. This fluency has probably taken them decades to learn, yet they have had only a few years' practice with the language of business.

And in a way that is simply human, Russians sometimes find it hard to say 'I'm sorry, I really didn't grasp that idea'.

> "When I first started working in international business, my foreign partner and I were using the same words but giving them entirely different economic definitions. Things got so confused we tottered on the verge of breaking off our deal out of frustration."
>
> Vladimir Kvint, *The Barefoot Shoemaker*

> "*In helping Russians get a start with their small enterprises, I've often had to help them with a business plan, so they could show it to the banks and get some credit. They don't always find it easy, because there are such negative connotations to the word* plan...*Also, I've found that they dislike the word* project — *which appears to translate directly into Russian, but sounds very nebulous and unlikely to happen. So I've started to talk about the* programme *instead, and they seem to prefer it.*"
>
> British consultant

If you fly in to Moscow to make a presentation to your Russian staff, be careful if it's the same material you delivered last week in Chicago. Ask a Russian to check it through for any sticky bits of language.

PART FOUR

Culture and Commercial Context

"If I were again faced with the challenge to integrate Europe, I would probably start with culture. Culture is the context in which things happen; out of context, even legal matters lack significance."

Jean Monnet, founder of the European Community

"[Business success requires] forsaking a reliance on thick, Western-style legal contracts for more personal relationships, allowing more time for negotiations and ensuring that negotiating teams have sufficient grey hairs."

John Howell of Ernst & Young, *Understanding Eastern Europe*

13

Culture

ASIA

Mostly when westerners are critical of Russian character traits, or when they are finding the Russians charming and exotic, the behaviours they are condemning or praising are Asiatic ones. Custine:

> “*...for the customs of the nomadic races will prevail for a long time among the Slavs...*”

ENIGMA

Where one writer deals consistently with the bleak, patient, cautious Russian soul produced by the cold weather, another dwells on the concept of *proizvól* — tedium unrelieved, and then jumps to the opposite idea: *razmákh* — recklessness, exuberance, panache, verve, commitment, enthusiasm.

Yet another offers this as the key to the ‘enigma’ of Russia: for the Russians, these contradictions are the spice of life.

You pays your money and you takes your choice. Russia has always held a fascination for the West, in direct proportion to her inscrutability.

(Incidentally, when Churchill spoke of ‘a riddle wrapped in a mystery inside an enigma’, he was not speaking of Russia, but the future *action* of Russia — meaning Stalin’s intentions. Hardly the same thing.)

DUSHA

Dusha means soul, but a very Russian soul. Knowing that *dusha* exists permits the Russians to live with adversity, and to counterbalance their frequently-observed inferiority complex with a sense of superiority to others. Only Russians, and possibly some artists of the Picasso class, have *dusha*.

Some outsiders claim to believe in it and to sense it in operation, while some Russians pooh-pooh the whole idea.

KOMMUNALKA

Mir means world. It also means peace, and the ancient village commune — a complex extended family. Village commune meetings were often ramshackle affairs, but they seem somehow to have got things done. The *mir* has sometimes been held up as an ideal by social reformers.

A *kommunálka* is a Soviet apartment where you share kitchen and lavatory with strangers foisted upon you by the authorities. It has never been held up as an ideal by anybody.

When a young Russian gave the Pioneer salute, his five fingers were the world's continents, held just above the forehead to symbolise *the priority of the public over the personal.*

The *zeks* in Ivan Denisovich's work gang, in 20 degrees of frost in a Siberian prison camp, keep themselves warm, build a wall, and actually get some job satisfaction through the exercise of team spirit — the team against the weather, the team leader against the authorities, the team against the other teams, all the teams against the guards in the section. When it is necessary to compete against *another section* — in a race to get back to the camp gates in time for supper, the guards themselves are running too, and so become temporary team-mates of the zeks.

There is a yearning for participation in many Russians, a natural *esprit de corps*.

MODELS FROM THE GURUS

Hall

In the 1960s Edward T Hall wrote about cultural differences — at about the same time as Claude Lévi-Strauss was developing anthropological structuralism — finding underlying shapes and patterns.

Hall offered two crucial measurements for building a practical model of another culture's behaviour: context and chronism. So any culture is, to some extent, either

HIGH CONTEXT or **LOW CONTEXT**

and either

POLYCHRONIC or **MONOCHRONIC**

- **High Context** communicators suppose that the people they are talking to are wise to the context in which the message is set: *my listeners have a good idea what this is all about, and if they don't know they can guess*. So in High Context cultures ideas are not spelled out in detail. People depend to a great extent on facial expressions, body language, inflexions of the voice, eye contact.
- **Low context** communicators like to spell things out, and to have things spelt out to them. Sentences are completed. Only one person speaks at a time. Telephone agreements are confirmed by fax.
- In **polychronic** cultures, people answer the phone, drink coffee, transmit sign language to their colleagues, listen to your presentation, and think about lunch all at the same time. They get bored and restless if only one thing is happening.
- In **monochronic** cultures, timetables are respected and activities are carefully compartmentalised. One item at a time.

Hall finds the French to be High Context/Polychronic, and the Germans to be Low Context/Monochronic. He did not examine the Russians.

We interviewed half-a-dozen westerners living and working in Russia, and half-a-dozen well-travelled natives, and they were unanimous: the Russian culture is Low Context/ Polychronic.

It is the Polychronicity that makes things seem so shambolic; Russians are perpetually juggling their schedules.

Some of our informants were afraid that the Low Context appellation might be denigratory — a hint of slow-wittedness.

An Italian:

This only applies to the broad mass — who are as intelligent as any people anywhere, but perhaps a bit less volatile than us Italians. The Russian intelligentsia could probably be placed in the High Context quadrant.

An American:

All I ever talk about is business, and in those areas I try to spell things out pretty clearly, so that slows us down. I guess on subjects where they're more comfortable, they can be pretty High Context. They're more expressive than the Germans.

An Englishman:

With outsiders, perhaps — that's when they're noticeably Low Context. Once you start to get intimate with somebody, there's a lot more reliance on little hints and signals.

Trompenaars

Fons Trompenaars developed a framework from an earlier system of Geert Hofstede's (a fellow Dutchman). Hofstede did not include Russia in his researches;Trompenaars did, and Russians show up on several of his scales.

- Russians are more *particularist* than *universalist*. This suggests they are happy to bend rules to suit given circumstances. (Many expatriates working in Russia will tell you this is so.)
- Russians are *ascription-oriented* rather than *achievement-oriented*. They believe in 'behaving as suits you even if nothing is achieved', and attach quite a lot of importance to a person's family background. (Russians have a reputation for self-indulgence, and the *nomenklatúra* system, through which family influence is exerted, has been well documented.)
- They are *collectivist* in their decision-making, but tend to attach blame (for negligence or error) on an *individualist* basis. (This perhaps ties in with Soviet vaunting of the group ethos, and the almost casual Soviet punishment of the individual.)

Our Yevgenii's view on this

Nobody likes to be lumped together with 150 million other people. On the other hand, Yevgenii Mikhailovich accepts that the Russian Character exists within the Russian Culture, that it is complex, and that you, as a visiting business person, might occasionally be confused.

At school, he learned some lines from Fyodor Tyutchev (1803–73):

> *"With the mind alone Russia cannot be understood,*
> *No ordinary yardstick spans her greatness;*
> *She stands alone, unique —*
> *In Russia one can only believe."*

For our purposes, Culture is interesting mainly in the way it influences conduct in business. Culture provides the soil in which business grows. Business is the commercial context — the trunk and branches which bear (or fail to bear) fruit.

14

Commercial Context

In December 1994, Enrico Franceschini was chief of the Moscow bureau of *La Repubblica*. He wrote an article for *Delovie Lyudi* (*Business People*), a Russian magazine:

> ...the Kremlin has every reason to be pleased with itself. Russia now has a new constitution and a new parliament elected by a popular vote. The struggle between the executive and legislative authorities is in the past. The Russian economy has shown the first signs of improvement. Inflation is on the decline, consumption and foreign investment are on the increase, a construction boom is clearly visible and privatised shops are filled with all types of goods.... Yet...this normality is chaotic and closer to quiet abnormality... . Tens of thousands of Russian factories have not paid workers for months. Intercompany debts are enormous: they now amount to 113 trillion roubles. Industrial production has declined by 25 per cent since 1993...Russia's 1994 harvest was the worst in the last 30 years.... Although government measures now support the rouble at just over 3000 to the dollar, a further decline seems inevitable. [It was.]

This 'normal abnormality' is of course a transitional stage — but what is the end point of the transition?

> "*What we will have will not be Karl Marx, but it won't be Adam Smith either.*"
>
> Russian industrialist

So check your own perceptions of what constitutes a 'normal' business environment. How much of that is just a set of ingrained habits in the markets you are used to? Prepare yourself for a very different style of behaviour in the emerging Russian markets.

LAW

In 1989, there was one lawyer for every 10,600 Soviet citizens — 25 times fewer than in America. Many western law firms set up in Russia to deal with the boom in business.

On 15 April 1995, the Russian government 'issued an order that effectively bars all foreign attorneys from advising clients on Russian law in Russia' (*Moscow Times*, 30 April). The foreign attorneys already practising in Russia did not immediately pack their bags. '...we need to take it a step at a time and see what it means, how to interpret it, and how it may be altered in the future.'

All the new laws in Russia are taking time to settle down and enter practice.

> “*...any analysis of recent Russian laws is likely to contain at least some predictive component.*”
>
> Frere Cholmeley Bischoff, 'Sources of Law',
> in *Doing Business in Russia*

Until the Gorbachev period, Soviet legal dictionaries ridiculed as bourgeois the idea that the state itself is subject to the rule of law. Since then, through constitutional changes and institutional innovations, Russia has lurched towards 'the Law-Governed State' — Franceschini's 'struggle between the executive and legislative authorities' being part of that process (*The War of Laws*, 1990–91). In other words, politicians and office-holders can no longer flout the law as much as they did.

For western business people, the common advice goes: Russia still lacks laws to protect investment; if you get into a wrangle with your Russian partner, negotiate, don't litigate. But try not to get into a wrangle in the first place.

The western partners in several showcase joint ventures have recently been in the newspapers, deliberating whether to slog out another round in the Law Courts, or cut their losses and let the Russian partners have the lot. (The Radisson Slavjanskaya hotel and the Arbat

Irish House store and bar were heavily featured in the press in 1995.)

It has always been a good idea to consult a Russian lawyer anyway — one who knows the corridors and the bureaucrats who dwell in them.

A Russian legal scholar:

> *"Even when good laws were adopted, there was an enormous gap between what the law said and how it was enforced. And in the gap is the bureaucracy."*
>
> Larisa Afanasyevna, cited in Yale Richmond, *From NYET to DA*

ADMINISTRATION

> Custine:
>
> *"In the Russian administration the minutiae do not eliminate disorder."*

Volokíta means red tape. Experienced expats in Moscow know how to deal with it: 'You build it into your business plan. If you were setting something up in the Sahara, you'd naturally take the sand into account when you made your calculations...'

And remember that the bureaucrats you meet are not stakeholders in your enterprise. Why should they want to help you succeed? There is an underlying idea that any activity which brings profit to a foreigner must somehow be leaving Mother Russia poorer — a zero-sum game.

MONEY

Marxist economics includes the concept *of the primitive stage of capital accumulation*. The phrase, with an ironic twist, has been given a new lease of life in post-Bolshevik Russia: what we are doing, smirk the crime barons and the *boyars* who have made themselves rich, is performing a necessary step in historical development as defined by Marx.

Under the old régime, leaving aside the military-industrial complex, the real work was done in the black economy, and capital accumulation has been taking place in the same spirit.

> “*...[The Mayor of Moscow said] from the outset that corruption was not only inevitable, it was laudable. It was the start of the transfer of money, the understanding of the value of money.... After all, had not many of the big names in America started out in an unsavoury business environment?*”
>
> John Kampfner, *Inside Yeltsin's Russia*

> “*A well-worn hammer-and-sickle emblem with the Cyrillic inscription 'Strengthen World Peace Through Labour' still clings fast to a projection of the St Petersburg Stock Exchange building. The new breed of capitalists in the city that gave birth to the Russian revolution is simply too busy for niceties.*”
>
> *St Petersburg News*, Winter 1994/5

'Niceties' might include accounting precisely for the money a Western bank has invested, or paying on time for a consignment of goods. At a seminar in London in late 1994, a seasoned international banker kept repeating over and over: 'Get 100 per cent payment in advance'.

> “*We don't have a bad debt position in Russia. Our distributor there is also our debt collector, and although I've heard no reports of physical violence, the style is undoubtedly heavy:* You owe us money and you will bring it to my office at noon tomorrow...”
>
> Western branded-goods producer

A note on bribes: Some Westerners say they do it all the time; some say it has never been necessary; some say they just give a Russian a budget to get results, and never ask him how he spent it. This is perhaps part of what people mean when they talk of the importance of having a local consultant.

TAXES

Onerous and byzantine. Many companies find that their tax liabilities, strictly computed, would be greater than their income — what the *Financial Times* calls 'a clearly unsustainable position which is solved by evasion'.

Sometimes legitimate avoidance is enough. The joint venture Russtel changed its name to Rustel — to avoid a 1 per cent tax on gross revenues imposed on ventures whose names include derivatives of the name 'Russia'. (Great tax, that.)

Some estimates have placed at 40 per cent of profits another levy on Russian enterprises — mob protection money. (Angus Roxburgh, in *Europa*, 1994)

NETWORKS

An important idea running through this whole book is that the key to business success in Russia is in *relationships*. Many Russian management consultants are, in effect, *relationship brokers*.

> "There are five networks in this town. There's the old senior *party* network, running stable enterprises — the big factories, really. They shade over into the *mafia*, who run the illegal operations. In turn, they might rub shoulders with the old Soviet *traders*, who form a network including the import-export bureaucrats and the managers of high street shops. Then there is the network of *scientists*, who are suffering because they know they have something of value, but have no idea how to bring it to market. Finally there's the old *komsomol* network: for the last ten years of its life, the komsomol wasn't full of dim party hacks — it was a training ground for young businessmen. I'm in with both the scientist and komsomol networks — that's how I make a living."

ETHICS

All observers agree that the key resource in Russia is the highly educated labour force. Yet more than one Western investor has found that they need training in good business practice: one big problem seems to be that they put friends before profit.

In *How to Profit from the Coming Russian Boom*, Richard Poe tells the story of Joe Francis, who set up a joint venture hairdressing salon, and succumbed to pressure to take on two woman managers from the old state-run Soviet salon.

"Those ladies hired 11 administrative people when we only needed two or three. I asked why do you need them, and they said, well, we have people, we have friends who needed jobs, so we gave them jobs. I told them it's got to change, and they said it's not going to change."

The English consultant:

"They set themselves up in a small business — a photo-processing franchise is popular. Six months later you go and say hello, and you find they're overstaffed already — unnecessary machine minders working two-hour shifts. It's a personalised form of social conscience. They hate seeing friends out of work."

PART FIVE

Yevgenii Mikhailovich

Yevgenii Mikhailovich Ivanov, 45 years old, is an invention.

We made him 45, because Russian insiders reckon 45 to be the cut-off point: any older than that, and there will be too much deep Stalinist conditioning. Much younger, and...

> *"we don't really have too much trouble. I made a point of recruiting young, undestroyed people."*
>
> Swedish executive, Moscow

Also your author is 45, and that creates a bit of empathy.

What have been the experiences of our composite Russian, our borderline Stalin-victim? How have they affected his outlook?

15

Education

EARLY YEARS

A lot of little Zhenya's time was spent playing with the other children in his *dvor* — the communal courtyard at the foot of his block of flats. Swing, seesaw, hide-and-seek.

From six months to three years, a crèche was available, and from then a kindergarten *détskiy sad* (children's garden).

> "*The first thing to strike us was the warm, welcoming atmosphere — created physically by the richly decorated walls depicting familiar fairy-tale characters, and emotionally by friendly, smiling teachers.*"
>
> Valerie Chamberlain, *Britain-Russia*, December 1993

> "*...the crushing group identity of kindergarten; the teachers are maternal and intrusive, and even parents seem to guard children from their own individuality — even from the most harmless flights of fancy — with instinctive fear...*"
>
> Colin Thubron, *Among the Russians*, 1983

As *Sputnik* was launched (1957), Yevgenii was in his first year of school. As well as his intellectual advancement, the education system concerned itself with citizenship, moral development, and character building — *vospitániye* (upbringing).

> "*It is a big room with three rows of desks, a portrait of the Leader on the wall behind the teacher's chair, a map with two hemispheres, of which only one is legal. The little boy takes his*

seat, opens his briefcase, puts his pen and notebook on the desk, and prepares himself to hear drivel.”

Joseph Brodsky, *Less than One*

During the 1960s, while Western education was becoming ever more liberal, Yevgenii was being taught to pursue excellence in conventional, traditional ways. All work was graded, and he was expected to get fours and fives. The classroom atmosphere was deferential. There was more negative criticism than positive encouragement.

A young Russian Jew emigrated to America with her family, at the end of her secondary education in the 1960s. Not surprisingly, she finds against the Soviet style of teaching:

“...Soviet schoolchildren, while usually ahead of American students in knowledge of their subjects, are much less likely to be able to think for themselves and to have their own opinions.”

Cathy Young, *Growing Up in Moscow*

Elsewhere, she expresses a common Russian doubt about the ‘soft’ ways of American teachers:

“...the mildest criticism...provokes resentment in both children and parents. Of course it is hideous to humiliate a child who has made an error...but why go to the opposite extreme, to the point where you almost can’t tell a child he’s doing something wrong for fear of discouraging him or ‘hurting his feelings’? How will a person so raised ever cope with criticism — or with real life, for that matter?”

A Western manager watching Yevgenii Mikhailovich bawling out a member of his staff would find it a bit hot and heavy. Conversely, Yevgenii might raise an eyebrow at the Westerner's way of delivering a reprimand — suspecting weakness and hypocrisy.

As a manager, Yevgenii would sometimes like to see a little more verve and creativity among his staff. He regrets that their initiative has been stifled to a great extent by their upbringing. Nonetheless, he values their technical expertise and respects the educational system that delivered it.

"My daughter has been at school here for a year. She is fourteen now, and they are entering her for the 'A'-level in maths, alongside 18-year-olds."

Russian mother in London

LITTLE OCTOBRISTS, PIONEERS AND KOMSOMOL

- **Age 6–9:** the *oktyabryáta*, instilling hard work, honesty and happy communal living. Star-shaped badge with a photo of chubby baby Ulyanov — Lenin. Virtually all children were enrolled as a matter of course.
- **Aged 10–about 14:** the *pionéri* were officially '...fighters for the communist cause...a love of labour and knowledge...formation of the younger generation [ie the *oktyabryata*] in the spirit of communist consciousness and morality.' Red neckerchief. Most early teenagers.
- **Aged 14–28:** *kómsomol* (Young Communists' League). Party training ground, labour pool for major industrial/agricultural projects. About half the young population.

Yevgenii took his first trip abroad — Bulgaria — with a *komsomol* group. A lot of his business contacts — the informal infrastructure — come from those days.

(He did not join the Communist Party. Only a small minority did.)

ARMY AND SPORT

Yevgenii reached military age (18) at a busy time for the armed forces. He knew people who were sent to Czechoslovakia after the 1968 repression, and others who spent an uncomfortable two years on the Chinese border after the Ussuri River incidents of 1969.

Yevgenii got off lightly, being an excellent volleyball player and playing for army teams — more travel around the Soviet Empire. The late 1960s saw a great flowering of interest in sport — increased leisure, more disposable income, government investment in facilities. (Quite apart from the propaganda value, a fit nation was ready for military endeavour: G.T.O. — *Gotóv k Trúdu i Oboróne* — Ready for Labour and Defence.)

Yevgenii still coaches his factory's volleyball team. He was disgusted by the 1989 revelations of drug-taking and payola among Soviet sports stars.

He is similarly shocked by the decline of the armed forces, and the epidemic of racist bullying in the former Red Army.

He had always felt that Russian sporting and military prowess were bright spots. He hopes they will be again. He enjoys talking about sport.

FURTHER EDUCATION

Yevgenii opted for science. In his generation, as part of the overall militarisation of society and of the Space Race, science was well funded by the government, and relatively immune to the numbing ideologification that was heaped upon Russians in other walks of life — a refuge.

Physics was tops (giving the Soviet Union six of its seven Nobel Prizes), and was centred upon the closed cities — centres of research and development for sensitive industries. Yevgenii's home town was one such.

Yevgenii is afraid that Russia will slip behind — become dependent on the scientific knowledge of other nations. Young people nowadays, he feels, revere traders and bankers where they once venerated scientists.

16

National Pride

THE WAR

Yevgenii grew up surrounded by reminders of Soviet victory in the Great Patriotic War (1941–45) — a victory won at inconceivable human cost.

> "...*the shared suffering of the war became a national myth under communism, held by many scholars of the Soviet Union to have been the main ideological prop of both the party and the state.*"
>
> *Financial Times*, 6 May 1995

> Yevgenii now is unhappy that *Russian* nationalism is being manipulated by the 'red-brown' politicians — the neo-fascists. He frankly prefers the emphasis to be on the *Soviet* victory in 1945.

HERITAGE

The Soviet régime did what it could to bring glory upon itself by reference back to Russia's past cultural achievements. But although they left a heavy bootprint on the literature, art, architecture and cinema of their own time, minister Zhdanov and his cronies failed to hijack the past.

The direct enjoyment of a painting, a symphony, or a ballet could not be tampered with by the Party. Good editions of classic works of literature, always produced in tantalisingly small quantities, were snatched up from the bookshops very quickly.

Yevgenii, a Russian baby-boomer, was part of a generation that turned on to Western rock music, and American literature. Yet they retain their pride in the achievements of Russian musicians, writers and artists.

Yevgenii does not consider himself a heavyweight intellectual or aesthete, but he believes good kitchen table talk should take in the world of books and cinema.

THE WORLD OUTSIDE

From Khrushchev's time onwards, the best perk in any job a Russian might get was the chance to travel abroad. Yevgenii's best so far (in terms of shopping, anyway) has been Finland.

For those who stayed at home, information about the world outside was consistently manipulated. *MIR* (peace/world/commune) was the aim of all Soviet policy, apparently. In this version of events, the Western powers were the aggressors, and the border guards were there to frighten spies away, not keep defectors in.

When Yevgenii was a teenager, the TV documentaries on life in America were (a) rare, and (b) heavily biased in favour of race riots and drug addicts sleeping rough. He was amused to see the TV reportage in the early 1990s: a tour of the gadgets in an American kitchen, for example.

Although Yevgenii was disturbed by '1984', and saw its relevance to Soviet life, he does not consider his own mind to have been polluted by anti-western propaganda.

Sometimes his older colleagues express xenophobia, in private among themselves and also at the negotiating table.

RUSSIA'S IMAGE

Yevgenii was too young to understand anything about the 1956 Hungarian uprising. Over Czechoslovakia 1968 he had mixed feelings — The Prague Spring was not much celebrated in the Soviet media, and he was just a volleyball-playing teenager.

He was very uncomfortable about Afghanistan, and the US-led boycott of the 1980 Olympic Games. The break-up of the Soviet empire and then the USSR itself were part of the same process — corroding Yevgenii's confidence in Russia, and her standing in the World.

As for the image of the government and the Party, Yevgenii's political education through his twenties took place in the world of Brezhnev — of whom one joke ran:

Brezhnev: I asked for a 40-minute speech! This lasted 2 hours!
Speechwriter: I gave you three copies...

In micro-economic terms, Yevgenii and his friends were ever aware of what David Remnick calls 'the sheer crumminess of the things that you could find...the decrepitude of ordinary life'. Brezhnev seemed to fit in with all that.

Yevgenii now finds it difficult to believe in senior politicians and their promises. He knows that things are in a mess.

With friends, he will enjoy a good moan about the sloppy way things are run, but he does not like to hear outsiders' negative comments.

Proverb: My country might be a rotten dungheap, but it's *my* rotten dungheap.

17

Economic and Social Life

MUDDLING THROUGH — WITH A LITTLE HELP

Yevgenii's parents had a hard time, and they wanted him to live in prosperity. Millions of other parents felt the same, and their emotions found expression in the golden era (or, more modestly, the 'thaw') of Khrushchev — the late 1950s and early 1960s. Famines became mere shortages, large plants were set up to produce small family cars, and treats were allowed.

Yevgenii is an only child, like many of his generation. (The family apartment was short on space.) There was a big fuss on his birthday, and family celebrations at New Year. Through connections, his father Mikhail Sergeevich rented a room for two weeks each summer in a house near Riga. (Yevgenii now finds it strange that he needs a passport and foreign currency to visit the Baltic republics.)

When he started earning money of his own, in his middle twenties, Yevgenii had enough spare cash to buy an occasional cassette of rock music — Chicago, Genesis, Led Zeppelin.... This inevitably brought him in contact with the harmless end of the black market, although he limited his dealings with the *fartsóvshchiki* (wide boys), whom he found distasteful and threatening. (He knows some of them now as successful businessmen.)

His career progress was not fuelled by desire for more money; there was little to buy with it. Status and power were more important, achieved through a perverse refusal to be beaten by the system.

> Yevgenii wants the future for his daughter to be more prosperous, just as his parents wanted a better life for him. He dislikes the more crass aspects of materialism which he sees around him nowadays, but knows that success in a free enterprise system is Natasha's best bet by far.

Yevgenii's perverse refusal to be beaten by the system meant that he had to be involved in dealings *na lévo* (on the left).

Getting materials to build a rudimentary one-room dacha, acquiring a pair of cross-country skis as a gift for Natasha, or fiddling a consignment of lubricating oil for the factory — all these required relationships and trading power.

Yevgenii looks to the young to transform the Russian way of making things and trading things, but he does not himself feel like a superannuated parasite. For some time to come, to make things happen in Russia will require his brand of entrepreneurship.Yevgenii counts himself very lucky not to be spending his evenings and weekends moonlighting as a van or taxi driver in one of the firm's vehicles.

FRIENDS AND ACQUAINTANCES

- *Drúzhba* is real friendship.Tradition has it that you need to consume a *pood* of salt with somebody before he can be your *droog* — friend. (1 *pood* = 16 kilogrammes). No favour is too much, and repayment can be deferred indefinitely. Things being what they are, favours among friends are what keeps society going.

Yevgenii knows some politicians who can get a case presented to central government. (The standing of a regional governor depends very much on how good a deal he gets for the region, and in Yevgenii's region that means getting a good deal for the local industrial base.)

Otherwise, under the Soviet system, his most important contacts were *up* the supply line. His sales side was much easier — delivering to the military. The quality had to be good, but the sales were guaranteed.

These days, there are some new telephone numbers on his list: those who can help him to raise capital for modernisation, or bring his goods to market.

- *Znakómie* are acquaintances, and without a network no business is done. That said, entry into a network depends on making contact at the personal level; you have to be liked and accepted as a person.

WORK: LOYALTY AND MOTIVATION

Yeltsin made it very plain in the early 1990s: 'We must *work*'. Without the protestant ethic, without experience of individual responsibility, without reliable systems of long-term reward for consistent effort, what will persuade the Russians to put their shoulders to the wheel?

The group

Russians value *sobórnost'* — togetherness. The idea is built into the forms of worship in the Orthodox church, and was of course meat and drink to the communists. There was little privacy in the communal sleeping hut in a village in ancient Rus, and precious little in a communal apartment in a Soviet town — where each family had its own toilet seat hanging on a peg on the wall of the shared WC.

Communal effort for the communal good was more lauded than individual competitive urges, all through Yevgenii's life. (Russians find it hard to understand why Americans find this sinister.) Given the right kind of leadership, a team of Russians can be world-beaters.

> *"That's how a gang runs. The authorities couldn't get a prisoner to work even in working hours, but a gang-leader could tell them to work in the break, and they would."*
>
> Alexander Solzhenitsyn, *One Day in the Life of Ivan Denisovich*

Authority

Traditionally, Russians have loved the trappings of power. Count the telephones on the General Director's desk; count the medals on Brezhnev's chest. Western bosses sometimes find themselves with inflated titles on their Russian business cards — so that the Russians who report to them can have grand-sounding titles in their turn.

Traditionally, Russians have respected and even loved strong national leaders with a direct emotional appeal — Stalin being the outstanding example. The millions who volunteered for the front in 1941–2 did so for Stalin and Motherland, not Lenin and the Party. There were scenes of great anguish when the murdering old tyrant died.

Traditionally, Russians are uncomfortable if they are given too much freedom. (Dostoevsky was much exercised by this, especially in *The Brothers Karamazov*.) In Yevgenii's lifetime the drab Brezhnev years, with the apparatus and its rules in full maturity, were politically and socially the most tranquil of all periods of Soviet history. They were also deeply cynical years, for by now the Russians had had enough of high-sounding messages.

Yevgenii would advise :

If, as a Western manager, you want to get real effort from your Russian staff, don't give them a lot of stuff about corporate vision, don't delegate too much authority, and don't expect them to say 'thanks for the challenge'. Suspend your own need to be liked.

Exert power from above, and set clear, measurable boundaries. Find an early opportunity to show that these boundaries are serious. Then give your staff latitude to get things done their own way, as a group, within the defined limits.

Give short-term rewards, and give them incrementally. This will develop the working habit.

WESTERN PRODUCTS, WESTERN WAYS

In the Brezhnev era, a packet of Marlboro was a handsome, slightly *risqué* gift. Many Russians believed that, through some accident of birth, most Americans were millionaires.

In the last decade, Marlboro has become a commonplace, along with Snickers chocolate bars, Heinz ketchup and Uncle Ben's rice. And the westerners are very visible in the cities — paying hotel bills that boggle the Russian imagination.

Russians who visit American supermarkets, once the initial bedazzlement has passed, have started to ask: does anybody really benefit from a choice of 29 varieties of pre-packed breadcrumbs?

And these successful business people who come to Russia to teach us how business is done: how admirable are they as individuals? Are they profound, well read and interested in people, or shallow, ignorant and interested only in their own profit?

D [*An Englishman*]: What do you think of Americans?

S [*A Russian woman*]: I don't know any. But my friends who do say they are...simpleton, fool.

D: That's a slightly sweeping judgement. They are very successful...Maybe one has to be a bit foolish to be successful.

S: But you mustn't have only money in your heart, it's bad.

Russia is still closed in upon itself. Communications with the outside world are poor. As a society they preferred — since they could not afford both — to put the First Man into Space rather than give everyone extra shoes. So they are not materialistic. And yet — they are totally hooked on the frippery of Western consumerism, any old bit of crap with I LOVE NYC on it.

Duncan Fallowell, *One Hot Summer in St Petersburg*

Yevgenii likes Western goods that are well made, and looks forward to the day when his factory's output can compete on equal terms.

As for the personal merits of the Westerners he meets, he judges them case by case.

"Every time I go to Russia, it strikes me afresh: these are highly educated and cultured people. Poetry, classical music, serious cinema — they all remain big draws among 'ordinary' people, who appreciate them in a very informed way. They're streets ahead of most western manager-types..."

Manager, Pierre Smirnoff Company

PART SIX

Negotiation

Equipped with a little better understanding of Yevgenii, we travel with him overnight by train to his home town, where negotiations will take place at his factory.

- Over a bottle or two, a cross-cultural conversation with a fellow traveller: what is the culture gap and how does it affect business relations? A case study.
- Then some advice on the real-time skills — Timing, Tactics and Talk.
- Finally, how to handle the Toasting when the deal is struck.

18

Cross-cultural Conversation

On the train to Nizhnii Novgorod, a Canadian businessman, Harry, falls in with the company. His bottle of rye goes on the table alongside Yevgenii's vodka, and after a couple of shots, he tackles Yevgenii (now Zhenya) on Russian ethics and business style. Yevgenii offers his perceptions (*in italics*) as we eavesdrop.

LAW BEFORE FRIENDSHIP

'Let me ask you a question, Zhenya, a hypothetical question. Let's suppose you're travelling in a friend's car — he's driving — and you're over the speed limit. Doing, say, thirty-five in a twenty-mile-per-hour zone...'

'That would be seventy instead of forty, approximately? Kilometres?'

'Right. And he hits a pedestrian — guy steps out in front of him. Both legs broken, weeks of treatment, and the case comes to court. You're the only witness. Now my question is: what would you say about the speed he was doing? Under oath, would you lie to protect your friend?'

'Am I under oath now, Harry? A vos amours.'

'Na zdorovie! Come on — do you cover up for him?'

'What punishment does my friend face?'

'Could cost him a lot of money. But let's say he's mainly afraid of losing his driving licence — needs it for his work, wife and kids to support. Do you want to know their names?'

'What's so funny?'

'I always get the same reaction when I try this on Russians: they bring it down to the personal level. Back home in Canada, people are much more ready to say *the law is the law.'*

'And friendship?...Where should we have our loyalty? To some impersonal law, or to a friend — with all his human failings? And what about The Law — is it there to protect people from each other? Or should people band together to help each other live in spite of the rules and regulations? Your law-abiding Canadians grew up in a benign system — in Canada people would expect that the wife and kids would be clothed, fed and housed, whatever happened to the driving licence. Maybe this grand attitude to truth is the prerogative of people in a rich, free, stable society...certainly you won't buy much beefsteak for your children — or keep your friends — if everybody else is lying from necessity, while you're standing up for truth.'

'So you'd feel obliged to testify that old Sasha was only doing thirty-five?'

'Obliged, no. As a good Russian, I would have to imagine the pitiful condition of his hungry children before I could come to a mature decision about Right and Wrong. Probably I would lie to protect my friend Sasha; after all, punishing him isn't going to repair the victim's broken legs, is it? ...You know that's been one of the problems dealing with the mafia? Some of our courts now have a jury system. So there we have our criminal, up in the box...box?'

'Dock.'

'Thank you. In the dock is a gangster, a murderer, a rapist. The state prosecutor has presented plenty of evidence, and for everybody's sake the jury should find this guy guilty and have him thrown in prison. He gives them a sorrowful stare, and turns towards his family on the public benches. Tears, moans, every kind of drama — for the jury's benefit. Not guilty.'

'And another nail in the coffin of law and order. These Russian attitudes can make it hard for a spoilt, naïve outsider — like me — to do business here. You know what they say? Once the contract is signed, *then* the Russian starts to negotiate...if you ever get that far...'

19

Harry Presents a Case Study

'The first time I came to Russia, back in '92, I was with a delegation of innocents just like myself.

'We were way over in Eastern Siberia, trying to set up a joint venture with a big fishing enterprise — and I mean big. About 30,000 employees. Great fish, lousy Soviet-era packaging. Anywhere outside the old Soviet bloc, no supermarket or deli would have it on the shelf.'

'I can imagine. And Russian consumers themselves are probably becoming a little more fussy?'

'The ones who can afford smoked salmon, yes. But mainly, I think, the management in Kamchatka had an eye on export business. They found it easier to conceive of new markets in terms of export, and earning hard currency — rather than finding new demands right on their doorstep. They wanted to package the stuff nicely, and sell it in large volumes to somebody who would market it outside Russia. Simpler that way.'

'All those years of Soviet experience. It's the smart way to do things in a supply-side economy. Prices are fixed centrally, quantity is more important than quality, and profitability, if it's measured at all, is measured by the ton.'

'I've learned a lot about the accounting systems since then, but remember this was my first visit. I was the money man in a North American delegation that came to work out a deal. On our side, a good-as-new suite of packaging machinery, various financial sweeteners and, as a bonus, training for some of their people in management and marketing. As I said, they had plenty to learn. We would set up seminars for them our side — somewhere they would enjoy, with good shopping and nightlife.'

'That would certainly be attractive to them. What's the word? "Junket"?'

'Don't worry about it — it's standard procedure everywhere. "Let's have the conference in Barbados!"'

'How did they react to the idea of you knowing more than them about these things — management and marketing? I hope you weren't heavy-handed — we have our pride, you know...'

'I'd like to say we were the soul of sensitivity, but in fact the negotiations never got that far...'

'So this is a disaster story?'

'There were a lot that year, I gather. Anyway, I'm getting ahead of myself...another shot of whiskey?...So that was what we were bringing to the party. On their side, they would be offering us a foothold in an enormous market.'

'And a lot of fish. Tell me about the people on their side.'

'As it turned out, there was only one person who mattered. The General Director. 24 years in the job. We'd done some homework, and we knew that the whole enterprise was being unbundled and privatised in various forms — fishing fleets one way, warehousing and distribution another. Our actual joint venture partner was to be the canning operation, and the managers there were very cooperative in the first day or two — showing us the plant, the harbour, the town.'

'They were the same managers as before privatisation, of course...'

'Yes, and it showed. They didn't seem to distinguish between "firm" or "company" — meaning the business — and "factory". *Zavód,* is it?'

'That's right. You've identified an important symptom. You don't change people's attitudes and perceptions by legislation. After twenty years running a Factory *under* The Plan, *you can't suddenly start thinking in terms of* profit centres, margins *and* the bottom line.'

'All that seems obvious to me now, but I found it disturbing then. I was talking a different language, wasn't I?'

'Oh, they were probably familiar with the words — from books and business magazines. But you have to understand the concepts quite deeply before you trust yourself to make a decision based upon them. They haven't gone that far, and it means that you and they will naturally look at any given situation in different ways. I hope I'm not lecturing...'

'I'm understanding how much work I have to do to get round to their point of view...'

'You have been living *with these ideas all your life — even your decisions about family life are made on the basis of* cash flow forecasts, *I imagine. It's second nature to you. These managers you were meeting were not* managers *in your understanding of the word. They were like the governors of provinces in some ancient empire — each fleet, each factory was run like that. The East Siberian Fish Industry Empire.... How did they react when you started talking about finances?'*

'They looked uncomfortable, even shifty sometimes. Changed the subject, steered the conversation back to technical matters where they were on familiar ground. It was clear they were marking time until Mr Big made his appearance.'

'I can well believe it. But in any case, what was your hurry?'

'I know what you're saying. We had told ourselves in advance that we must be patient, and adjust to the local rhythm. I mean, I've worked in South America and India...we were bursting to get down to business, but we tried not to let it show. I'm Canadian, but I get to be labelled "pushy Yank" everywhere I go. Anyway, the Emperor arrived on the third day, and things started to go badly wrong. Looking back on it now, I can see there was an enormous gulf in perceptions.'

'He was polite to you, no doubt?'

'Formally, yes. But he didn't behave like the head of a corporation setting out on a Win:Win negotiation. More like Brezhnev than Gorbachev.'

'I can imagine the atmosphere. Might I suggest that Mr Big was a little bit afraid?'

'He didn't seem afraid — he was coming across like the man who's holding all the cards.'

'Afraid of being made to look silly in front of his subordinates, perhaps? He knew that at any moment you might start talking business jargon to him, and that it would be very difficult for him to follow you. I imagine he had personally appointed all the people in responsible positions beneath him. He ruled through them by ukáz *— by* diktat. *It's natural that he would be afraid of losing his dignity in front of them.'*

'You're right, of course. And that partly explains why he spent more time with the other delegation — people who spoke his language, and manoeuvred in the same ways. They were a group of Ukrainians who arrived on the same day, and they were interested in buying an old canning line — the one our equipment was supposed to be going to replace. As I say, old Boris Nikolayevitch paid them more attention than us. We were kept sitting in the minibus for twenty minutes at one point, while he went through some detail with the Ukrainians — and they all seemed to be smoking three cigarettes simultaneously.'

'So you're like the Germans. Only one thing at a time?'

'Cigarettes, you mean?'

'No, business meetings. We Russians enjoy complexity and contradiction, in some perverse way, and it's one of our ideas that an intelligent person should be able to hold more than one thought in his head at a time.'

'*Touché*. Simple-minded, that's us. Anyway, we spent a lot of the day just standing around and waiting. We joked about it and said maybe Boris just wanted us to have the great Russian standing-in-line experience. But we felt pretty uncomfortable, and the negotiation hadn't even started yet. Boris dropped us at our hotel, and refused to come in to discuss the agenda. We would meet the next day, and he already had a clear plan for the meeting. Next morning, the day's sessions got cancelled — the General Director had pressing business elsewhere.'

'Did you believe that?'

'Believe me, we discussed it all day. In the end, we had two competing theories: one, that it was some ancient Tatar negotiating technique to soften us up, and two, that he'd gone out and got drunk with the Ukrainians, and was now at home nursing his *pakhmélie*.'

'Perhaps you should have sent him some Alka-Seltzer.'

'What do you say, was it heavy-handed tactics, or the bottle?'

'Possibly both. Who knows? You arrived expecting to be treated like important clients, and by now, you were feeling like second-rate salesmen. Again, that's a result of all those years of Centrally Planned Economy. The supplier had the power, so the idea of being terribly polite to your customer is very radical. We don't really know how to do it, yet. What happened when you finally met across the table?'

'Three on our side, eight on theirs. The usual row of grey suits. They would hear our proposal. We went into our rehearsed presentation, starting with the advantages to both sides — possible market segmentation, production flows, and how we thought the money should be handled. I realise now that it was all too much for them to digest at once. Silence when we finished, and then Boris spoke up.

'Need it be said? He had a quite different perception, and we had a lot to learn. Calculations had been made on the basis of current Russian tax laws, and the action on the JV was to be split 71–29 in the Russians' favour. The same ratio would apply to the Board of Directors — although in fact the Russians would run everything without us, and we could come over once a year to rubber-stamp their decisions. Our main contribution was to be installation and technical training.'

'At that time he was quite right, of course — operations on Russian soil had to be run by Russians. We're gradually learning to be more flexible.'

'Well, we were trying to decide how to respond to all this. Was Boris staking out a tough initial bargaining stance? How should we respond? Then he made it plain that we weren't really negotiating at all. He said that he now had experience of three successful joint ventures with foreign enterprises, including one last year with the Japanese — so he knew how to go about it.

'Step One was that we all sign a standard Company Charter, and Step Two was a Formal Agreement — details as already made clear. To help us understand what these documents would entail, we were given examples to take away and study in our hotel that evening.'

'Are you beginning to understand the significance of pieces of paper? Lenin declared bureaucracy to be an enemy of progress, and through all the Soviet period it was the one aspect of government that we were all allowed to criticise — in general terms. In practice, one was always dealing with some guy who wanted a piece of paper to cover his backside. "If we follow the established formula, and have plenty of documents in the file, nobody can say we've done anything wrong."

'We were quite prepared for some fairly rigorous paperwork, sure. What we were given turned out to be copies of the documentation on the Japanese joint venture. We read with interest that they'd done a dream deal, buying millions of dollars worth of salmon over a four-year period and paying peanuts for it. Some extra fixing that was never recorded, wouldn't you say? Payments to the General Director's account, maybe?'

'Certainly a man in his position — a whale left high and dry on the beach, really — is tempted to organise a cosy retirement for himself. Think of him as a senior local politician, rather than as the head of a corporation, and then look at what happens among politicians in Italy, or India, or Great Britain. If you're doing million-dollar deals, don't you expect to meet this kind of thing? But I must say, I'm surprised they let you see the paperwork from the Japanese agreement.'

'So were we — and especially since there was a specific confidentiality clause in there. The papers and all details were supposed to remain secret for twenty-five years. We didn't think that said much for the trustworthiness of our negotiating partners.'

'I think perhaps Boris Nikolayevich was sending you a signal, saying that he not only expected to dictate the terms of the agreement, but also the rules of the game.'

'Changing them when it suited him.'

'In 1992, that's the way things were — and the way they will remain, to some extent, until the last of the old-style vlásti — the powers-that-be — *has retired.'*

'Well this one won't be putting any of *our* money into his Swiss pension fund. We went back the next day, and said we could not consider, on these terms, committing a million dollars' worth of plant. We needed a total re-think of the project — especially representation in decision-making, or no go. We had taken a deep breath and thought we'd said the final word — our bags were packed.'

'Did you actually walk out?'

'No, it was all quite calm. We suggested they might like to take a time-out, and they came back twenty minutes later with a proposal concerning the million dollars: that it would be better if we officially priced the machinery as worth much less than a million before we shipped it, so as to save on import duties. We hadn't got our message across. We were saying "it's all off", and they were asking us to get involved in shady dealings.'

'It's very difficult for the old vlasti *to grasp that outside investors come from a world with different rules. Boris would suppose that you and your superiors back home also got results by ignoring, or bending, the law. You know, don't you, that sometimes all the legitimate taxes on a piece of business add up to more than the business turnover? You just* have *to evade them, or you bankrupt yourself. How were Boris's subordinates behaving?'*

'The ones who'd been so welcoming to us three days before were beginning to look a bit embarrassed. We broke for lunch, and one of the other guys took the opportunity to tell me, in my capacity as financial expert, that somebody was lined up for the job of Financial Director of the JV. The daughter of some local politician, apparently. How do you say "nepotism' in Russian?'

'Same word — or more commonly we speak of svyázi *— connections. You know, it's quite possible she was well qualified for the job. These days, the children of the* nomenklatúra *are often first in line for places in the best business schools.'*

'I don't know what this woman knew about business, but she was no doubt plugged into the *svyazi*. Anyway I didn't like the idea that she was going to be dumped on us without discussion. In fact, the whole deal was dead in the water by now. We decided to cut our losses, put it all down to experience, and head for home. If I had to sum it all up, I'd say we'd tried to shape our idea as "good for our corporation and shareholders; good for your corporation and shareholders", whereas in fact we had been dealing with an individual.'

'In a way you got off lightly. Suppose you'd made a deal with Boris Nikolayevich, and then he'd been replaced. The deal you made with him might have had to be renegotiated from scratch with his successor.'

'What's the lesson there? How would you advise a neophyte to approach a negotiation in Russia?'

'Find a dependable and competent opposite number to negotiate with. Judge him by other deals he has done, and according to whether you think you can click with him, and keep up the personal understanding long-term. Then build a relationship with that person. After that, you just make up the rules as you go along.

'What was the mood as you left Kamchatka?'

'Incredible. Three of the guys drove us out for our flight to Khabarovsk. Right outside the airport building, they opened their briefcases and produced cognac and sausage, and we had a party...Do you have an interpretation?'

'They were feeling sentimental, and that's a good excuse for a party. Also perhaps they felt they had failed to make you feel welcome in the context of business, and were making amends by showing you hospitality as best they could.'

'That old Russian skill of making the best of a bad situation. And with that, I'm going to see if I can get some sleep. *Spokóinoi nóchi*.'

'Good Night.'

20

Notes on Real-time Negotiation

We are well on our way to building a model of the Russian business culture.

After a tour of Yevgenii's plant the next morning, you come to the negotiating table. What happens when the game starts?

When there is friction between two cultures doing business together, differing attitudes to *time* are often the cause.

Across a culture gap, we should adapt *our tactics* and be careful about interpreting *their tactics*.

And the rules of *talking* will be different — what we say and how we say it.

TIMING

We saw earlier how Edward T Hall's model finds the Russians to be *polychronic* — life a terrible jumble, poor sense of priorities, never on time; more like the Irish than the Swiss.

> *"I was running a ten-module management seminar — evening classes. At the end of module 4, I said, 'Next week we're looking at Time Management. Between now and then, could you please spend five minutes a day filling in this chart of how you're spending your time? It will be useful next week.' Next week, not one of the buggers had filled it in...out of a group of 36....."*
>
> British consultant in mid-air over Belarus

The dictionary will tell you that *seichás* means *now* and *'Seichas!'* means 'Right away!'. In practice it means something between 'Any time now' and 'Maybe'.

In the days of the Five-Year Plans, the targets would often be broken down into monthly chunks. Result: three weeks of torpor, followed by a great rush of work in the last few days; deleterious effects on quality of product.

Russians have greater reserves of patience than spoiled Westerners; they learned patience the hard way. They can bear waiting, and they are not reduced to nervous wrecks every time there is a bureaucratic setback. This gives them an advantage in negotiations.

It is a long-standing Russian joke that all Americans rush around all the time shouting 'Time is Money!'. What a strange idea... .

- Fix the agenda in advance.
- Allow time before the business for small talk and refreshments.
- When business starts, be prepared for delays and setbacks.
- Do not seem to be in a hurry.
- Display tenacity.

TACTICS

The Russian at the negotiating table knows he has something the Westerner wants — his minerals, his market, his signature on a deal... He is conditioned to believe that the Westerner is wealthy — has limitless resources. Why not go for the best deal he can get?

"I find it useful sometimes to take a step back, and ask: on this point, who's buying and who's selling? Who's feeling strong and who's running? And then I ask — is the other side seeing it the same way?"

Italian expatriate manager

"I said to Sasha, tell him he hasn't finished the job, and I'm not paying him till he's done something about all those trailing wires. Sasha said, you can't do that, not in Russia. And I said, just tell him what I said, so Sasha told him.

Next day he came back and ran ducts for the wires, and I paid him. Now I'm some kind of hero."

English management consultant

"**American negotiation:** *the first American says 10 and the second American says No. So the first comes down to 9.95.* **Russian negotiation:** *The first Russian says 10 and the second Russian says No. So the first comes down to 5. The Russians are fumbling; they don't really know the value of what they're trading; there's no market price to take as a benchmark....*

The real decision-maker — the one who understands the ins and outs of the deal — is not usually the senior man in the Russian delegation. It is important of course to show the boss proper respect, but you can ask at some stage 'is it you who will be drafting the contract?...ah...well perhaps it would be useful to meet the person who is...' Then you make a relationship with that person."

Russian management consultant

"*Westerners come here with written proposals, and the Russians look them through. 'Where's the cash? All I see here is a list of all the work we have to do!' A Western manager in a corporation can spend his whole professional life without dealing in cash. In his home life, he's surrounded by insurance policies and pension schemes and credit cards. Of course he's forgotten to mention cash in the proposal.*"

Senior Russian manager

"*Trust, but verify.*"

Ronald Reagan, using a Russian proverb to justify his stance on the Americans' right to inspect Soviet nuclear decommissioning

"*Negotiations...took 12 months, mainly because Amersham's [Russian] partners looked upon the process as a business course.*"

Case Study 3, CBI, *Doing Business in Russia*

> *"Compromise is native to America but not to Russia."*
>
> Yale Richmond, *From NYET to DA*
>
> *"The club...has a small restaurant, two bars, a sauna and a steam bath, all of which are perfect for business negotiations (Russian-style, of course!)"*
>
> Advertising copy, Metrospetsstroi Union
>
> *"Negotiating style? All I ever seem to get is 'contract on the table, let's go through it paragraph by paragraph...'"*
>
> American, six months resident in a Moscow hotel

- Be as ready as you can with documentation.
- Show a little steel early in the negotiation.
- Allow some emotion into the proceedings, and raise your voice if necessary.
- Take plenty of time-outs.
- Keep checking your assumptions.

TALK

Business talk

In an earlier section we identified Russian as a Low Context culture, in which people spell their ideas out clearly to each other. Nabokov wrote *Lolita* in English, and later rendered it into Russian — his native language. He preferred the English version, because English has 'the ability to flick at meanings in contexts where the Russian must be painfully explicit'.

We have also noted earlier that middle-aged Russians (like Hungarians, Poles and Czechs) came to the world of business late in life, and quickly get a headache from too much business-babble.

The interpreter might be an extreme case of this. Having devoted his professional life to learning foreign languages for literary and academic purposes, he has now been pressed into action as a commercial interpreter.

One story tells of the American who was negotiating for the purchase of several stores (high street shops), and found himself looking at a row of stores (warehouses) instead.

- Slow down and speak up and use simple terms and concrete examples.
- Keep checking that all is clear, asking for repetitions and read-backs.

(Older interpreters, incidentally, tend to favour the English form of English over the American.)

Social talk

You might hear them running Russia down among themselves, but Russians are sensitive; they easily begin to feel patronised.

"Did you hear Ambassador Strauss's little wisecrack? 'If I had ten thousand dollars to invest, I'd invest it in Russia. If I had five million dollars to invest, I'd invest ten thousand dollars in Russia.' Very funny, but we didn't like it."

Russian manager

Whatever you've read about prostitution and pornography in Moscow, Russians have a strong code of decency.

"I'm delighted to see things more open now, but I don't like all the sex and violence in the American films on television. In my younger day, we of course had our sexual episodes, but they were private — we didn't all run around shouting about it. It's open to question whether that's repression or just good manners."

Russian woman, university teacher, Yevgenii's generation

Forget about Ivan the Terrible and Brezhnev; Russians have a lovely sense of humour. They cherish Ivan the Fool (*Ivanúshka Durák*, or *Iván Durachók*), a low-born dimwit who somehow comes out on top; there is a long tradition of 'laughter through the tears'; they love jokes debunking authority figures. These three tastes in combination have made English film comedian Norman Wisdom ('Mister Pitkin') a national favourite.

- Don't be a know-all or a show-off.
- Offer advice with tact.
- Admire what you are invited to admire, and show respect to local customs.
- Don't use foul language.
- Let yourself be human, emotional, humble.

21

Celebrating

We have stopped short of a 'How to Negotiate' manual.

We cannot take our story of your negotiation with Yevgenii and his colleagues further, since we do not know who you are or what your business is. We choose, optimistically, to believe that the negotiations are a success, and that mutually profitable business is concluded, over a series of meetings in offices and restaurants (and who knows, in a *banya* or on a bear hunt).

Time to open a bottle!

WHAT DRINKING MEANS TO RUSSIANS

Custine:

> ...when the *muzhiks* get tipsy, these men, brutalised as they are, become softened, instead of infuriated. Unlike the drunkards of our country, who quarrel and fight, they weep and embrace each other. Curious and interesting nation!

Russians drink

> from grief and from joy, because they're tired and to get tired, out of habit and by chance...when they're under the influence people acquire a freedom that is unknown to non-drinkers — liberty, unprecedented equality and good-natured fraternity.

Lev Kopelev, *A Poet's Life*

Alcoholism is a serious national problem, susceptible to no direct treatment. Alcohol is built into the Russian social system, and apart from a short-lived abolitionist period in the 1920s, it was freely available through innumerable outlets at all hours. Add to this a dismal shortage of entertainment in a generally drab life. It is not really difficult to understand why Russians drink a lot.

Since the 1950s sales tax on drink has contributed between 10 and 14 per cent of total state budget revenues — or some 40 per cent of all direct and indirect taxes. *(Cambridge Encyclopedia of Russia).*

"More people are drowned in a glass than in the ocean."

Russian proverb

In the early 1980s, Russians over the age of fifteen averaged 11.5 litres per year of pure alcohol in state-produced beverages, with another 2–3 litres of home-produced hooch on top of that. Allowing for many groups who consume little — many Muslims, many women — this represented crisis level drinking among Russian men, and the government acted.

Gorbachev did himself no political good with his anti-vodka campaign, and years later recalled a joke from the time:

With supplies restricted, two Russians find themselves in a long, slow queue for vodka, and one gets fed up. 'I'm off to the Kremlin to kill Gorbachev!'.

Forty minutes later he's back. 'Did you do it?' asks his friend.

'No, I didn't. That queue was even longer.'

During 1987 and 1988, while the campaign was running, thousands of Russians died from drinking alcohol illegally derived from hair spray, boot polish, jet fuel.

Now the campaign is history, and annual consumption per head is running at about 6 litres.

Vodka and other spirits make up more than half of that.

> *"...local vodka, a source of national pride as Russia's main contribution to the wellbeing of nations, has been swamped by cheap imports and illegal products...more than half the vodka drunk in Russia now is imported or illegal."*
>
> *Daily Telegraph*, 9 February 1994

> *"Litres of vodka you can buy with the average Russian monthly wage: 1985–12; 1995–44."*
>
> *Guardian*, 8 March 1995

DRINKING AMONG RUSSIANS

When a group of friends get together to drink at home, or in the dacha, or at the campsite, there will be *zakúski* (snacks/ nibbles) on the table — salt fish, pickled mushrooms, sausage, cheese, crackers. The vodka is taken in gulps from a *ryúmka* (shot glass). The bottle(s) should be finished at a sitting — a habit compounded by the foil tops on many bottles of vodka, which are impossible to replace once torn off.

Efforts are being made, and may be taking hold in the younger generation, to change Russian drinking habits not through making cheap vodka difficult to get, but by making it smarter to drink good vodka in moderate quantities.

William Pokhlebkin, a Marxist historian of vodka, observes:

> *"...in the high, aristocratic milieu, the proper way of drinking vodka came to be defined. Vodka should be served cold, almost frozen, and drunk in small, barely perceptible mouthfuls."*

As the Scots are nationalistic about their whisky, so the Russians claim cultural ownership of vodka (the affectionate diminutive of *vodá* — water). In the early 1980s, the Poles provocatively claimed it was an 18th-century Polish invention...

"Shaken, the Soviet Ministry of Foreign Trade asked experts to prove Russia was *first. It turned for help to the Institute of History and the Higher Scientific Research Institute of the Fermentation Products Division of the Central Department of Distilling of the Ministry of the Food Industry. They failed."*

Financial Times, 7 March 1993

HOW TO DRINK WITH RUSSIANS

Stand-up cocktail parties are not really the Russian way. To celebrate, in public, Russians go out to a restaurant and drink-talk-drink-eat-drink-dance.

To some extent, yes, Russians like to ply their foreign guests with drink and see how they shape up, but it's not very serious and certainly not sinister.

A late-night conversation head-to-head over a bottle can be an important part of the bonding, but you don't have to get tearful or falling-down drunk.

Some people make excuses — *I'm driving*, or *I'm under doctor's orders*. Better if you can just be gently assertive. That's always supposing you don't just want to let go...

TOASTING

With larger groups, be prepared for toasting to take place. It will punctuate the meal, the quality of the speeches will be variable, and you will be a great disappointment to everybody if you don't propose a toast yourself — starting with a few quite formal expressions of gratitude and amity. Then allow yourself some elbow room, and talk about our children's children, throw in a reference to classical literature, and close with a slogan that won't be too hard for the interpreter to translate.

Peace and Friendship (Mir I Druzhba) is the classic, but what about *'Freedom and Profit'*, or *'Our Customers, and Their Customers'*, or *'To our Successors in this Joint Venture; may they have a Job for Life'?*

- No Russian will think the less of you if you let go a little — being sentimental, boisterous, human. A drink might help.
- All Russians will think more of you if you can show, without affectedness, some wider learning or understanding of the world and its culture.

PART SEVEN

Yevgenii at Home

You have to stay on for a couple of days while the ink dries on the contract, and to cement further the relationships you have been building — especially with Yevgenii.

He invites you to his home for the evening, to meet his wife Svetlana Alexandrovna, and his daughter Natasha.

This is the sort of thing you might pick up about Yevgenii's home life during a good evening.

And some idea of the ground a conversation might cover.

22

Yevgenii and his Family

HOME

Press the door buzzer.

Odd number of flowers, remember not to shake hands over the threshold. Good Evening.

Please come in... *What a lovely place...*

How do you do...*take your time over the name game, be sure to get it right...óchen' priyátno, Svetlana Valentinovna ...*

How pretty! Thank you...Natasha, please find a vase...Oh, it's up to you, of course, but if you would *like* to put slippers on...we sit in here...would you like to wash your hands ?...

The great impression is of warmth and Gemütlichkeit. *No stove, alas. Clever use of space. So actually this unlovely concrete edifice contains dozens of homes like this.*

Teenage daughter, having presented herself, has gone to her room 'to study', and might join us later. Yevgenii's raised eyebrows and Svetlana's sigh suggest Natasha is at a difficult age...

*Vodka and a spread of zakuski...*please, help yourself...*(don't forget there's a biggish meal to follow this)...a little more vodka...toast to* **'All the Hard Work We Did to Reach This Agreement'.**

WIFE, MARRIAGE AND WOMEN'S ROLE

Svetlana is a doctor. The administration and delivery of health care in Russia is very largely in female hands; the profession brings little status and pays badly.

She met Yevgenii in the late 1970s. They were at separate professional conferences in Moscow, and their delegations collided in the same big restaurant one evening. They danced, and found they had a home town in common... .

The flat they live in is close to the hospital; several neighbours are medical colleagues of Svetlana's. (Most of Yevgenii's colleagues live on the other side of town, closer to the plant,)

Natasha was born in 1979. Her upbringing was largely in the hands of her maternal grandmother, as her parents continued with their careers.

Svetlana has been aware of the broad feminist issues — the hospital where she works is a hotbed of discussion. Yet her experience as a wife in Russia has been full of *go-shopping-in-the lunch-break, carry-the-eggs-home-in-a-paper-bag-on-the-overcrowded-tram, help-Natasha-with-her-homework....*

Betsy McKay, in the *Moscow Times*, on International Women's Day:

> *"...nothing more than an excuse for men to absolve themselves of their dismal behaviour the rest of the year..."*

Yelena Kondakova, cosmonaut, holder of the female world record for time spent in space, tells of how she had to squeeze her training between driving their eight-year-old daughter to and from school and arriving home in time to prepare an evening meal for her husband.

Good Housekeeping magazine has just been launched in a Russian edition, with an initial print run of 150,000 copies.

DAUGHTER

Natasha has always been a good daughter. She likes books and plays the piano quite well. She is 16 now.

She doesn't remember the Brezhnev era — she was only a little girl. Her formative teens were spent in an atmosphere that was either (a) a greedy moral vacuum, or (b) a heady, upbeat time of change — depending on whose version you are reading.

Yes, she wants to study business, but doesn't really know the best way forward. There are so many institutes of this and that springing up, offering diplomas in 'Russian, English, two other languages, Literature, History of Religion, Bookkeeping, Customs Regulations, Production, Computing...'.

The crucial factor, both parents feel, is self-assurance. The intellectual, academic side of business is surely not very difficult; what *is* hard is to be assertive. If Natasha can learn that, there will be a future for her.

Talk of self confidence.

> “*You know the average Soviet person was known colloquially as a* sovók — *a dustpan, literally. Receptacle for rubbish. In Soviet society, anything that was not expressly permitted was implicitly forbidden. There was always some crushed little person in a uniform waiting to salve his own ego by criticising you, rubbing your nose in your own inadequacy. It was very difficult to grow up with self-esteem...*”

As the *zakuski* are put aside and the main course is prepared, a chance to browse along the shelves.

BOOKS AND RECORDS

Technical and medical reference books and dictionaries in Russian and English. Assortment of language courses, grammar books. Family encyclopedia. School books and children's picture books. An Italian recipe book in German.

A good sampling of Russian classics. It would be possible from this shelf to follow the 19th century's 'superfluous man' through from Lermontov (Pechorin in *A Hero of Our Time*), and Gogol (Chichikov in *Dead Souls*) through Turgenev's *Bazarov* and Goncharov's *Oblomov* to the wan country doctors in the plays of Chekhov. Existential anti-heroes a century before the French versions of Camus and Sartre.

A complete Pushkin, and a separate, illustrated edition of *The Bronze Horseman.*

Western classics in translation (and one or two Western editions): treasured from childhood — *Peter Rabbit, Winnie the Pooh, Alice, Treasure Island*; and adolescence — Jack London, Alexandre Dumas; some more serious tomes that might or might not have actually been read — Dickens, Thackeray, the Brontes, George Eliot, Galsworthy; some that clearly have been read — O Henry, Steinbeck, Salinger.

Along the spectrum of dissidence: early Solzhenitsyn, Akhmatova, Pasternak, Brodsky, later Solzhenitsyn.

On a mixture of vinyl and cassette: Svetlana's classical collection; some Russian jazz of the 1930s (her grandfather's); a few American and British rock classics from student days; some contemporary Russian popular music (*Did you know Alla Pugacheva has sold 200 million records*?). Natasha's heavy metal is in her room, and she listens to it on headphones.

DINNER

Spicy chicken Georgian style, sweet pastries, and a bottle of Bulgarian red.

- Talk of food.

  "When they voted for an end to communism, many people were really voting for an end to queueing. There is more in the shops now, but the prices of good things have gone through the roof. A university friend of mine married a Colombian man she met who was in Moscow studying telecommunications, and went to live with him in Cartagena. Her first letter talked of nothing but the fruit she could buy in the market..."

- Talk of Russia and her future:

  "Will things get better for the majority of Russians? Yes, but not the way things improved in America in the forties and fifties, or Japan in the sixties and seventies. Over the next two decades, we can repair ourselves and get back on our own Russian track — which is not to say we are ungrateful for your advice..."

- Will something of the true Russia survive these changes?

  "Yes, of course, just as it has survived seventy years of Bolshevism. It is perhaps old-fashioned to speak of dusha *— the Russian soul, but...another glass of this...?"*

PART EIGHT

Phrasebook

A functional set of phrases for handling meetings, making presentations, negotiating, and socialising afterwards.

MEETINGS: PARTICIPANTS
ДЕЛОВЫЕ ВСТРЕЧИ И ИХ УЧАСТНИКИ

Self-introduction	**Знакомство**
My name is *Smith, John Smith.* Pleased to meet you.	Меня зовут Смит. Джон Смит. Очень приятно познакомиться.
How do you do. *Smith's* the name, *John Smith*	Позвольте мне представиться. Я - Смит, Джон Смит.
Representing...	**Представляя Компанию**
I represent *company x* / *department y* / the interests of *group z.*	Я представляю компанию X/ отдел Y/ интересы деловой группы Z.
I'm here on behalf of *x/y/z.*	Я являюсь представителем и действую от имени X/Y/Z.
Contributing	**Вступая в беседу**
May I put a word in here, *Mr/Madam* Chairman?	Позвольте мне добавить несколько слов, Господин / Госпожа председатель.
Perhaps this is where I come in.	Полагаю, что я должен высказать свою позицию по этому поводу.
Fighting for Space	**Отстаивая свою позицию на переговорах**
May I interrupt/ butt in/ ?	Разрешите мне перебить...
If I could get a word in edgways...	Позвольте мне вставить несколько слов...
Emphasising a Point	**Подчеркивая главное**
It's very important to realise that...	Очень важно понять, что ...
The vital point here is:...	Принципиально важный момент здесь, это то что...
Correcting a Misunderstanding	**Устраняя взаимонепонимание**
Perhaps I didn't make myself clear. What I was trying to say was...	Возможно вы меня не поняли. Я хотел сказать, что ...
I'm sorry if that was a bit vague/obscure/confusing. I meant...	Извините, я выразился немного непонятно / смутно / неопределенно. Я имел в виду, что ...

Proposing a Motion	**Делая предложение**
I propose the following: '*x...y...z...*'; perhaps we can put it to the vote?	Я предлагаю следующее: 'X,У,Z.' Давайте поставим это предложение на голосование.
Shouldn't we take a vote on this? I'm prepared to propose the motion.	Почему бы нам не проголосовать за мое предложение ?
Welcoming Another's Contribution	**Благодаря за полезные советы**
Thank you for that, *A*, it was very useful/ interesting.	Спасибо, это очень полезное / интересное замечание.
I think we should all be grateful to *A* for that contribution.	Я думаю, мы все должны быть благодарны А за его предложение / совет.
Verifying Another's Meaning	**Уточняя позицию собеседника**
I'm not sure I follow. You seem to be saying...	Я не уверен, что я вас понял. Кажется, вы сказали ...
Let me see if I've got this straight: your position/ idea seems to be...	Позвольте мне убедиться в том, что я понял вас правильно. Ваша позиция / Ваша идея в том, что ...
Giving Support	**Поддерживая собеседника**
I agree with what you're saying; please go on.	Я согласен с тем, что вы говорите, пожалуйста, продолжайте.
Precisely! You've hit the nail on the head.	Абсолютно верно, вы попали в самую точку.
Disagreeing	**Не соглашаясь, возражая**
I'm afraid I can't agree with you.	Боюсь, я не могу с вами согласиться.
That doesn't make sense; I'm against it.	В этом нет смысла. Я против.
Throwing New Light	**Новый подход к проблеме**
Perhaps we should try looking at thc question in a different way...	Может быть, нам следует посмотреть на этот вопрос с другой стороны.
There's one aspect that we haven't considered yet...	Существует еще один аспект, который мы не рассмотрели.

Offering a Suggestion	**Предлагая решение проблемы**
May I offer a suggestion at this point?	Позвольте мне сделать предложение по этому вопросу.
It's only a thought, but why don't we...?	Почему бы нам не ...
Asking for Clarification	**Просьба объяснить что либо**
Could you repeat/ re-frame that? I didn't quite catch it.	Не могли бы вы повторить, я не совсем понял.
What was that again? I'm a bit slow today.	О чем вы говорите? Я не уловил вашей идеи.
Dropping the Idea	**Оставляя рассматриваемую идею**
Let's just forget the whole thing, shall we?	Давайте забудем об этом, вы не возражаете?
Why don't we just drop it/ scrap it/ shelve it?	Почему бы нам просто не оставить / не закрыть этот вопрос / не отбросить эту идею?
Conceding a Point	**Соглашаясь с точкой зрения собеседника**
I accept that you have a very good point.	Я соглашаюсь с тем, что ваша позиция хорошо обоснована.
I'm forced to admit that you're quite right .	Я вынужден признать, что вы вполне правы.
Inviting Comments	**Приглашая к обсуждению**
I'd like to know what everyone else thinks about this question.	Мне бы хотелось знать, что остальные думают по этому вопросу.
Can we throw it open at this point, and pool our ideas?	Возможно, следует оставить вопрос открытым и обменятся идеями.
Checking Another's Purpose	**Уточняя цели собеседника**
What's behind that comment?	Что скрывается за вашим предложением / обьяснением?
What are you getting at exactly?	К чему именно вы стремитесь?

Calling a Break
Shall we stop for a break/ adjourn for a while?

Объявляя перерыв
Не объявить ли нам перерыв / не прерваться ли нам на какое-то время?

Let's take a time-out / a breather / a pause for thought.

Давайте передохнем / устроим перерыв.

MEETINGS: THE CHAIR
ВЕДЕНИЕ ПЕРЕГОВОРОВ

Opening the Meeting
I would like to open the meeting now.

Начиная переговоры
Я предлагаю начать переговоры.

Shall we get down to business?

Не перейти ли нам к делу?

Purpose of the Meeting
The reason we've come together today is:...

Цели переговоров
Мы сегодня собрались здесь для того, чтобы...

Let me remind you what we're here for:...

Позвольте мне отметить, что мы собрались для того, чтобы обсудить...

Welcoming Guests
May I welcome to the meeting *Mr A*, who is here to...

Приветствуя гостей
Позвольте мне представить вам Господина А, который...

I am happy to see that *Dr B* has joined us.

Мне очень приятно видеть, что Доктор В нашел возможность присоединится к нам сегодня.

Dealing with the Minutes
Can we agree the minutes of the last meeting?

Ведение протокола
Все согласны с протоколом последних переговоров?

I will ask the secretary to read the minutes.

Я попрошу секретаря прочитать протокол переговоров.

Beginning the Agenda
The first item on today's agenda is...

Приступая к повестке дня
Сегодня первый вопрос на повестке дня ...

The first thing we have to raise/ discuss/ agree today is...

Первый вопрос, который нам предстоит обсудить / решить / поднять, это...

Referring to Documents	**Ссылаясь на документы**
I hope you have all had time to read the report/ paper.	Надеюсь, все имели возможность ознакомиться с отчетом / документами.
Let me draw your attention to page 7/ the financial section.	Позвольте мне обратить ваше внимание на седьмую страницу / на финансовую часть документа.
Giving Someone the Floor	**Предоставляя слово кому-либо**
I'll hand over to *Mr A*...	Я предоставляю слово Господину А.
I now call on *Ms B*, who I know has something to say...	Сейчас я предоставляю слово Госпоже В, которая, как я знаю, хочет высказаться.
Curtailing a Contribution	**Прерывая выступающего**
Perhaps I could stop you there.	Позвольте, я прерву вас здесь.
I'm afraid time is rather short; could you make your point?	К сожалению, у нас мало времени, не могли бы вы сформулировать свою идею короче?
Thanking a Contributor	**Благодаря за выступление**
I'm glad you brought that to our attention.	Я очень рад, что вы привлекли наше внимание к этому вопросу.
A very useful contribution, I'm sure we all agree.	Я уверен, все согласятся с тем, что это было очень полезное замечание / выступление.
Reverting to an Item	**Возвращаясь к обсуждавшемуся ранее**
Can we go back now to item *x* on the agenda?	Не могли бы мы вернуться к вопросу х нашей повестки?
I think we should turn back to what was said earlier...	Я думаю, нам следует вернуться к тому, о чем мы говорили раньше.

Restoring Focus	**Акцентируя внимание на главном**
We shouldn't forget the purpose of this meeting: we are here to...	Нам не следует забывать о цели наших переговоров, мы здесь для того, чтобы...
We're drifting from the point; can we get back on course?	Мы отходим от основного вопроса повестки, давайте вернемся к нему.
Postponing an Item	**Откладывая обсуждение вопроса**
Could we postpone/ put back our discussion of this item until...?	Не стоит ли нам отложить обсуждение этого вопроса до...
Perhaps we could come back to this later.	Возможно, стоит вернуться к этому позднее.
Maintaining Order	**Обеспечивая порядок**
Order, please! Could we have *one* meeting?	Пожалуйста, соблюдайте порядок переговоров.
This is getting us nowhere. Let's try to have a proper meeting.	Такое обсуждение нас ни к чему не приведет. Постарайтесь, пожалуйста, соблюдать порядок на переговорах.
Offering a Summary	**Подводя итоги**
Perhaps I could sum up the discussion so far:...	Возможно, я могу подвести некоторые итоги обсуждения.
It boils down to this simple issue/ fundamental question:...	Итоги обсуждения приводят нас к простому выводу / фундаментальному вопросу.
Going for Consensus	**Достигая общего согласия**
I think we are generally agreed that...	Полагаю, в целом мы все согласны, что...
Can we take it on a general 'aye' that...	Итак, основное большинство за то, чтобы...
Voting	**Голосование**
We should now vote on this/ a show of hands, I think.	Думаю, нам следует проголосовать / поставить вопрос на голосование.
In favour...against....carried/defeated by 7 votes to 5.	За...против...принято / опротестовано семью голосами к пяти.

Any Other Business?	**Есть ли еще вопросы к обсуждению?**
Have we covered everything?	Все ли вопросы были нами рассмотрены?
Could I ask for any last-minute matters you want to raise?	Есть ли еще вопросы к обсуждению?
Drawing to a Close	**Заканчивая переговоры**
I'll close the meeting now.	Переговоры закончены.
I declare the meeting closed.	Я объявляю переговоры оконченными.

PRESENTATION
ПРЕЗЕНТАЦИЯ

Starting	**Начало**
I've been asked to speak to you today about...	Меня попросили выступить сегодня на тему...
I'm here in my capacity as expert on...	Я выступаю сегодня здесь как специалист по вопросу...
Route Map	**План презентации**
This will last *x* minutes, during which we will consider *x...y...z...*	Презентация рассчитана на X минут, в течение которых мы рассмотрим X, У, Z.
Perhaps you could keep your questions until the end.	Я попрошу вас задать все возникающие по ходу вопросы после окончания презентации.
Categorisation	**Анализ проблемы**
The subject breaks down into three categories/ areas of research:...	Обсуждаемый вопрос распадается на три части / подвопроса ...
We will consider this subject/ technique under three main headings:...	Мы рассмотрим этот вопрос / эту технологию по трем основным направлениям.

Finding the right level

Уровень обсуждения проблемы

I know you are all in the picture, so I'll skip the basics.

Я понимаю, что здесь люди сведущие, поэтому я опущу всем понятные основы проблемы.

I won't blind you with science; this will be easy to follow.

Я не хочу запутывать вас научными терминами, я постараюсь объяснить доступно.

Opening a Paragraph

Приступая к раскрытию проблемы

Turning to the subject of...

Обращаясь к вопросу о ...

The next aspect to consider is...

Давайте рассмотрим следующий вопрос, касающийся ...

Closing a Paragraph

Заканчивая рассмотрение проблемы

That's all I have to say about *x*.

Это все, что я хотел сказать по этому поводу.

So much for *y*, for today at least.

По крайней мере, на сегодняшний день тема исчерпана.

Data: Approximating and Summarising

Работая с цифровыми данными и результатами

In round figures/ broad brush strokes, it looks like this:...

Округляя цыфры / грубо говоря, результат выглядит следующим образом.

And here is the bottom line/ the result we've worked out:...

Итак, мы можем подвести итоги / Это результаты, которые мы получили.

Visual Aid

Применяя наглядные пособия

To bring this idea to life, we have produced this illustration.

Для наглядного подтверждения идеи мы используем данную иллюстрацию.

I hope this diagram will help you to grasp/ lodge/ recall the idea.

Надеюсь эта диаграмма поможет вам понять / уяснить эту идею.

Diagrams: Features	**Диаграммы**
This shows the principle/ workings in a flow chart/ floor plan.	На этой диаграмме / таблице проиллюстрированы выводы / показан процесс рассуждения.
As you can see from this drop in current/ surge in demand...	Как вы можете видеть, на таблице данное снижение / рост спроса ...
Graphs: Trends	**Графики - иллюстрация тенденций**
upward/ downward	Тенденция повышения / снижения ...
steady/ erratic	стабилизации / неустойчивости ...
climbing/ rising/ going up	скачки / подъемы / рост ...
falling/ dropping/ going down	падение / снижение / движение вниз ...
gently/ steeply/ dramatically	незначительно / ступенчато / значительно ...
flattening out	выравнивание ...
peaks/ troughs	пик / минимальное значение ...
underlying trend	основная тенденция.
Tables: Analysis	**Анализ таблиц**
If we compare *x* with *y*...	При сравнении X с Y ...
reading across/ down the columns...	анализируя таблицу по рядам / по вертикали ...
setting *y* against *z*...	положение Y относительно Z ...
breaking this down into factors/ various outputs...	разбивая таблицу по факторам / итогам / результатам ...
the variations between *z* and *x*...	расхождение между Z и X ...
significant patterns emerge.	определяем закономерности.
Drawings: Simplification	**Рисунки как простая форма доказательства**
This is simple/ crude/ rough-and-ready, but it expresses...	Этот набросок прост / весьма приблизителен, но он иллюстрирует ...
Here's an outline sketch to support the argument.	Здесь представлена иллюстрация в поддержку приведенного доказательства.

Analogy
Let's take *xyz* as an analogy/ think of it in *xyz* terms.

Аналогии
Давайте рассмотрим XYZ аналогично / подобно ...

You might find this easier to grasp if we draw a parallel with *xyz*.

Возможно, вам проще будет понять идею, если мы проведем аналогию / сравним ее с XYZ.

You-appeal
Let me point out what *xyz* could mean to you.

Это специально для вас!
Разрешите мне заметить, что для вас XYZ значит ...

In your situation, I would be particularly attracted by *xyz*.

На вашем месте меня бы особенно заинтересовало XYZ.

Expressing Enthusiasm
I believe very strongly in this idea/ proposal/ equipment.

С энтузиазмом об идее
Я глубоко верю в эту идею / предложение / оборудование.

I have no hesitation in recommending *xyz* ; it's great.

Я не имею никаких сомнений в рекомендации XYZ для использования - это замечательная идея.

Inviting Questions
No doubt you have some questions...

Задавайте вопросы, пожалуйста
Без сомнения у вас возникли некоторые вопросы ...

I'll be happy to take questions now.

И сейчас я буду рад ответить на ваши вопросы.

PROPOSALS
ПРЕДЛОЖЕНИЯ

Position
As I see it, the present situation is this:...

Позиция
Насколько я вижу, настоящая ситуация такова, что ...

Let us consider where we are now, and where we want to be.

Давайте рассмотрим наше теперешнее положение и то, чего мы хотели бы достигнуть.

Problem
Now we come to the key issue.

Проблема
Теперь мы подошли к основному вопросу.

That means there is a problem to solve, and I define it like this:...

Это означает то, что у нас есть проблема, которую предстоит решить, и я бы определил ее как ...

Possibilities	**Возможности**
There are several options open to us/ which we can rule out:....	Несколько возможных решений открыты для нас. / Некоторые моменты необходимо исключить.
On grounds of economy/ urgency, we should consider/ forget....	Из соображений экономии / срочности вопроса нам следует рассмотреть /забыть о ...
Proposal	**Предложение**
So I am sure you can see that the best way forward is...	Итак, я уверен вы видите, что нам следует ...
And that brings us to my recommendation:...	По указанным причинам я бы рекомендовал ...
Scope	**О размерах предложения**
Our proposal embraces the following elements:...	Наше предложение охватывает следующие пункты ...
We have chosen to bid for these portions of the contract:...	Мы решили работать над следующими частями контракта ...
Good Intentions	**С наилучшими намерениями**
We have made our best efforts with this bid, and hope you approve it.	Мы надеемся, вы одобрите наше предложение, мы приложили все усилия, чтобы сделать его привлекательным.
We see this as the beginning of a happy and fruitful relationship.	Мы рассматриваем это как начало нашего взаимовыгодного и плодотворного сотрудничества.
Emphasising Quality	**Подчеркивая качество**
You will not find a better/ more reliable product anywhere.	Не думаем, что вы найдете где-либо лучший продукт / более надежную аппаратуру.
We pride ourselves on delivering the very best.	Мы горды тем, что поставляем только самое лучшее.
Emphasising Profitability	**Подчеркивая прибыльность**
The installation will pay for itself in *x* months.	Данная установка окупит себя уже через х месяцев.
This investment is a machine for making money.	Такая инвестиция подобна станку для печатания денег.

Explaining High Price
We know the price is high, but that reflects the exceptional *xyz*.

О высоких затратах
Конечно цена высока, но она отражает исключительные качества X, У, Z.

The price does not seem so high once you take *xyz* into account.

Если принять во внимание X, У, Z, то цена не выглядит слишком высокой.

NEGOTIATION
ПЕРЕГОВОРЫ

Getting Their Full Shopping List
It would be useful to have a complete list of what you have in mind.

Составляя полную картину предложения
Было бы неплохо, если бы вы представили полный перечень того, что вы предлагаете.

Can we be sure there will be no hidden extras/ last-minute demands?

Можем ли мы быть уверены, что в последнюю минуту вы не предъявите какие-либо скрытые экстратребования?

Links between Factors
As you know, we must take *x* into account; it ties in with *y*.

Взаимозависимости
Как вы понимаете, X тесно связано с Y, поэтому необходимо принять во внимание так же и X.

The *y* factor will be crucial, since it affects *x* and *z*.

Y фактор имеет принципиальное значение, так как он тесно связан с X и с Z.

Probing Priorities
Why are you so adamant about *x*?

Уточняя приоритеты
Не объясните ли вы, почему вы так упорно отстаиваете X?

I don't see why you attach so much importance to *y*.

Мне не совсем понятно, почему вы придаете такое значение Y?

Checking Their Decision Power
Does the final decision rest with you?

Проверяя возможности собеседника принимать решения
Имеете ли вы право принять окончательное решение?

Are you the final arbiter on this, or will you need to consult/ refer back?

Будете ли вы принимать окончательное решение, или вам необходимо посоветоваться?

Remaining Hypothetical	**Воздерживаясь от обещаний**
For the time being, all these suggestions are provisional.	На сегодняшний день все наши предложения являются условными.
Nothing is agreed until everything is agreed, I'm afraid.	Боюсь, мы ни о чем не договоримся, пока не обсудим все детали.
Showing Steel	**Проявляя твердость**
Let me say before we go any further that we cannot accept...	Позвольте мне сказать до того как мы перейдем к следующим вопросам повестки, что мы не можем согласиться с ...
Certain items are non-negotiable, like...	Определенные вопросы не подлежат обсуждению, такие как ...
Expressing Disquiet	**Выражая беспокойство**
I'm not entirely happy about...	Мне не совсем нравится то, что ...
There's one thing troubling me. Could we look again at...?	Меня беспокоит один вопрос. Не могли бы мы вернуться к обсуждению ...
Finding Common Ground	**Находя общие интересы**
I'm sure we have this need/ goal/ interest in common.	Я уверен, что у нас есть общие потребности / цели / интересы.
This is where we both stand to gain.	Данное предложение является взаимовыгодным.
Minor Matters	**Дела незначительные**
I think we can dispose of *x* quite quickly.	Я думаю, что мы сможем решить этот вопрос довольно быстро.
We won't let this item *y* detain us long.	Это не займет у нас много времени.
Making Offers Conditional	**Ставя условия**
Our agreement on this point *x* will depend on what happens with *y*.	Наше соглашение по поводу Х будет зависеть от У.
If you will yield a bit on *y*, then we can meet your needs on *x*.	Если вы сможете нам немного уступить, тогда мы согласимся с вашими требованиями по поводу Х.

Tentative Acceptance
It's beginning to look rather attractive.

I sense we are on the right track.

Соглашаясь предварительно.
Это начинает выглядеть довольно привлекательно.

Я вижу, мы на верном пути.

Rejection
I'm afraid we can't possibly agree to that.

No, I'm sorry, but that just won't do.

Не соглашаясь
Боюсь, с этим мы никак не можем согласиться.

Нет, мне очень жаль, но так дело не пойдет.

Bargaining
Shall we start looking for trade-offs and compromises?

Perhaps it's time for a bit of give-and-take.

Торгуясь
Не следует ли нам пойти на компромисс?

Мне кажется сейчас время пойти друг другу на уступки.

Squeezing Their Offer
I'm sure you can do better/ go up higher than that.

Is that really the best you can come up with?

Добиваясь своего
Я уверен вы можете улучшить свое предложение / пойти дальше.

Неужели это лучшее, что вы можете мне предложить?

Resisting Pressure
I must insist on this point/ be quite firm about this.

There is no room for manoeuvre here.

Не поддаваясь давлению
Я вынужден настаивать на этом / проявить здесь твердость.

Здесь не может быть никаких изменений.

Stimulating Movement
Perhaps you can suggest a way out of this deadlock?

I'm beginning to sense progress; can we take another step or two?

Движение к цели
Можете ли вы что-либо предложить, чтобы выйти из этого тупика?

Я чувствую, мы начинаем добиваться определенного прогресса, не пойти ли нам дальше?

Meeting in the Middle
We are prepared to meet you half-way on this point.

Shall we split the difference?

Уступая друг другу
Мы готовы уступить, но при условии что и вы сделаете скидку.

Давайте разделим между собой разницу в цене.

Verifying Agreement
If we can just check the details, we seem to have an agreement.

Подтверждая соглашение
Полагаю, что мы достигли согласия, осталось только проверить детали.

I think that's a deal, then. Could we just swap notes?

Думаю, мы договорились. Надо только обменяться замечаниями.

THE SOCIAL GATHERING
ОБЩЕСТВЕННЫЕ МЕРОПРИЯТИЯ

Calling for Attention
Could I have your attention for a moment...?

Обращаясь к собранию
Могу ли я на несколько минут привлечь ваше внимание ...?

If I could, I'd like to say a few words...

Если вы мне позволите, я бы хотел сказать несколько слов ...

Marking the Occasion
As you probably know, today is important because...

Повод к собранию
Как вы знаете, сегодняшний день является особенным для нас ...

Today we celebrate ...

Сегодня мы отмечаем ...

Introducing Guests
Do you two know each other? A, this is B
B, I'd like you to meet A.

Представляя гостей
Кажется вы незнакомы? Это Господин B.
Мне бы хотелось представить вас Господину А.

Allow me to introduce my friend/ colleague...

Познакомьтесь пожалуйстазта мой друг/ коллега...

Self-Introduction
Let me introduce myself. My name's..., and I'm a friend/ cousin of ....

Представляя самого себя
Разрешите мне представиться. Меня зовут ..., и я друг / двоюродный брат ...

I don't think we've met. Does the name John Smith ring any bells?

Думаю мы незнакомы. Возможно вы слышали обо мне, я - Джон Смит.

Re-establishing Acquaintance	**Мы, кажется, знакомы**
I remember you! It must be years! Hello again!	Конечно я помню вас! Сколько лет, сколько зим! Здравствуйте!
You'll have to remind me, I'm afraid. I know your face, but...	Извините, боюсь что я не помню ваше имя. Ваше лицо знакомо мне, но ...
Offering Drink	**Предлагая напитки**
May I offer you a drink? What can I get you?	Позвольте мне предложить вам что нибудь выпить. Что вы предпочитаете?
Let me top you up.	Не хотите ли вы выпить?
Refusing Drink	**Отказываясь от предложения выпить**
That's very kind, but no thank you. Perhaps a soft drink/ juice?	Это очень любезно с вашей стороны, благодарю вас. Но я предпочел бы только воду / сок.
I'm doing fine with this one, thank you.	Нет, спасибо, не беспокойтесь. Я уже налил себе воды / сок.
Offering Food	**Угощая**
Would you like some salad/ dessert?	Не хотите ли салат? Пожалуйста, попробуйте этот десерт.
You really should try this; it's a local speciality/ a seasonal dish.	Вам действительно стоит попробовать это блюдо. Это особое блюдо национальной кухни.
Taking Your Leave	**Прощаясь**
It's been a lovely evening, but I really must be going.	Это был замечательный вечер, но я действительно должен идти.
Goodness, is that the time? I must be off!	Боже мой, уже так поздно! Я должен идти.

PART NINE

Как это делается на Западе

Культура бизнеса, адаптация к новым условиям, консультанты по вопросам управления, навыки презентации, техника ведения переговоров, проведение совещаний.

Как это делается на Западе

ДАВАЙТЕ ПОЗНАКОМИМСЯ, Я — ДЖЕК

Большая часть этой книги представляет из себя попытку познакомить западного бизнесмена со взглядами на жизнь, привычками, традициями русских. Для того чтобы показать каким образом эти привычки и традиции воздействуют на поведение русских бизнесменов мы использовали вымышленный персонаж по имени Евгений Михайлович Иванов.

Следующие несколько страниц мы посвятим бизнесмену с Запада во многом схожему с Евгением Михайловичем - они родились в один день, выросли в счастливой и довольно-таки обычной семье, оба получили образование одного уровня и занимают значительный пост в крупном объединении. Давайте назовем его Джек, это имя является разновидностью имени Джон, и это имя встречается наиболее часто среди мальчиков рожденных в 1950-м.

Для нас не имеет значения в какой фирме работает Джек.

Не имеет значения и какой пост он занимает, кроме того, что надо сказать что по делам служебным ему приходится общаться с русскими бизнесменами. Возможно он является специалистом по маркетингу, или контролирует финансовые операции фирмы, или же выполняет обязанности производственного инженера ('Мастер на все руки').

Его национальность также не имеет значения. Мы не можем рассказать здесь о культуре бизнеса применительно ко всем без исключения национальностям, представители которых вам могли бы встретиться, но мы можем описать их общие черты.

Мы расскажем об особенностях делового общения Джека. О том что представляется наиболее важным: как он воспринимает проблемы в бизнесе и как формулирует решения, как он аргументирует свою позицию и как доводит ее до собеседника, как он устраивает сделку и как обсуждает ее, как он участвует в переговорах и как он ведет их. А так же деловой жаргон, который он использует.

Мы рекомендовали западному бизнесмену попытаться лучше изучить и понять русскую культуру и приспособиться к ней.

Если бы и вы - русские так же попытались применить к своему собственному стилю некоторые из идей, изложенные на следующих страницах, тогда, как знать, Евгений Михайлович и Джек могли бы весьма преуспеть в совместном бизнесе.

Международная культура бизнеса

Точно так же как итальянец может еще говорить и по французски, владея двумя языками, Джек освоил вторую культуру бизнеса которая необходима ему для ведения дел с иностранцами. Его иностранные партнеры поступают также.

Такую культуру ведения бизнеса вы можете наблюдать в холлах международных аэропортов, в залах для проведения конференций гостиниц Марриот а также на страницах западной прессы например в разделах о бизнесе в газете Франкфуртер Аллгемайне.

Язык международного бизнеса

Английский язык является языком международного бизнеса. (Извините, Франция, Испания и Китай.) Но это своего рода диалект английского, который сформировался для простоты и ясности в общении - ограниченный словарный запас, простая в использовании грамматика, упрощенные идиомы.

(Например, если бы Джек использовал русский язык для ведения бизнеса с китайцами или с греками, он не стал бы заботиться о тонкостях использования глаголов совершенного и несовершенного видов. Такие слова как 'контракт' или 'совместное предприятие' использовались бы в их беседе естественным образом, в отличие например, от использования названий грибов или многочисленных прилагательных описания заката солнца.

Литература

Это большие, толстые книги о стратегии менеджмента, о тенденциях развития мировой экономики, о стиле руководства и самосовершенствовании. Написанные знатоками своего дела в Бостоне, Токио и Лондоне, эти книги сформировали определенную концепцию международного бизнеса, почти идеологию, они позволили управляющим почувствовать себя профессионалами.

(Джек ждет и покупает эти книги как только они выходят из печати или читает сокращенные варианты в журналах о бизнесе.)

Факты

Портативные компьютеры, модемы, Золотые Карты международных авиалиний.

(Часто пользуясь услугами крупнейших авиакомпаний, Джек после определенного количества полетов сможет бесплатно отвезти своих детей в Диснейленд.)

Приоритеты

Сотрудничество, а не конфликты, взаимоотношения на долгосрочной основе, а не легкая и быстрая прибыль, влияние на людей, а не контроль над ними.

(Джеку немного надоели псевдонаучные термины которыми принято выражать эти идеи, но в рамках здравого смысла он согласен с ними. Сегодня алчность и жажда быстрой наживы восьмидесятых позади.)

ПЕРЕМЕНЫ - САМОЕ ХОДОВОЕ СЛОВО

Вы наверняка встретите западного бизнесмена в России, и это результат фантастических изменений которые происходят сейчас там.

Последние 20 лет и особенно в течение нынешнего затянувшегося экономического спада слово *перемены* находится в центре внимания большинства западного менеджмента.

Усердие предпринимателя является реальной движущей силой любого нового растущего бизнеса. Зрелый же бизнес выживает и процветает приспосабливаясь к изменяющимся обстоятельствам.

Надо заметить также, что, к сожалению, зрелый бизнес склонен к расстройствам, связанным с его возрастом. Это излишний персонал, склеротизм и бюрократия, заторможенность и консерватизм. Подобная организация приспосабливается к переменам с трудом. И когда обстоятельства изменяются с драматической скоростью, как это происходило в последние 20 лет, управляющий персонал и рядовые сотрудники такой фирмы вынуждены находить оправдания тому что они не принимают этих изменений.

“Такая новая технология не повлияет на то как работает мой отдел.”

“Этот всеобщий спад является временным и представляет лишь часть естественного цикла.”

“Конкуренты, появляющиеся в других частях мира, не являются соперниками на нашем рынке.”

“Наши клиенты останутся преданными нам до тех пор, пока мы в состоянии предложить им тот же старый, знакомый сервис.”

“Вероятно сокращения будут необходимы. Но к счастью я незаменим.”

Коротко говоря, организация ‘приходит к самоотрицанию’. (Использование терминов психологии стало общепринятым.

О бизнесе говорят почти так же как о пациенте, с его индивидуальной психикой.)

Таким образом, спрос на услуги ‘консультантов по переменам’ в нынешнем поколении велик. (То же поколение наблюдало рост спроса на услуги психотерапии.)

Джек имел дело с консультантами разного рода. Иногда он приветствует их помощь, но некоторые из них по его мнению являются шарлатанами.

Чем занимаются консультанты по вопросам управления

Многие консультанты работают в устойчивых, относительно неизменяющихся областях, таких как информационная технология, финансы, инженеринг. Здесь же мы рассмотрим деятельность консультантов в гибких, изменяющихся сферах.

- *Предвидение возможных изменений, работа коллектива как единого целого и принципы деятельности* — все это нацелено на определенные результаты и помощь персоналу в совместной работе по их достижению.
- *Перестройка организации бизнеса* — направленность на сокращение потерь и фокусирование совместных усилий там, где действительно следует, на обслуживании клиентов.
- *Системное мышление* — рассмотрение бизнеса в системной взаимосвязи с внешними, органическими факторами, влияющими на его состояние, а также со всеми присущими ему тонкостями.
- *Оценка персонала, включая психологическую оценку* — оценка способностей, квалификации и требований каждого отдельного сотрудника. (‘поскольку люди являются нашим главным ресурсом’).

- *Общее качество управления* — управление, обеспечивающее работу всех членов организации в одном направлении, и получение клиентом качественного продукта.
- *Обучение принципам руководства* — для руководящего персонала среднего звена, для тех кто обеспечивает эффективность функционирования ‘человеческого капитала’ (что практически совпадает с формированием коллектива, с влиянием на сотрудников, а так же с обеспечением мобильности организации, ее способности к изучению внешних изменений и приспособления к ним).
- *Наставничество* — психологическая и тактическая поддержка для отдельных менеджеров.
- *Перепрофилирование* — помощь в поисках работы сотрудникам уволенным в связи с сокращениями (в результате перестройки организации). (Перемены? Конечно же! Я знаю что это значит. Это слово означает что люди оказываются без работы.)

ФОРМУЛА ПЕРЕМЕН

Процесс перемен может быть сформулирован в виде формулы:

Н х В х Д > С

Что означает:

- надо взять величину вашей **НЕУДОВЛЕТВОРЕННОСТИ** нынешней ситуацией
- умножить ее на значение вашего **ВИДЕНИЯ** лучшего будущего, и

- на значение силы ваших **ДЕЙСТВИЙ** по достижению нужного результата.

Перемены произойдут если величина всех этих факторов вместе окажется больше чем **СОПРОТИВЛЕНИЕ** к изменениям.

(Заметим, что если какой либо из этих трех факторов равен нулю, то изменений не произойдет.)

Практически тоже самое происходит во время каждой успешной революции.

Для компании **НЕУДОВЛЕТВОРЕННОСТЬ** появляется как только прибыль начинает падать.

Картина **ВИДЕНИЯ** лучшего рисуется командой управляющих, и представляет из себя описание того как фирме следовало бы работать и с какими результатами.

СОПРОТИВЛЕНИЕ часто представлено консервативными, ленивыми или боязливыми руководителями заявляющими: 'У нас и без того дел хватает, какие еще изменения!', идущими иногда даже на саботаж новых инициатив.

Когда западные менеджеры говорят о 'коммуникации перемен', они имеют в виду такие действия как информация и вовлечение персонала в процесс изменений. ('выделение тех кто начнет и возглавит перемены', 'распространение информации о предполагаемых результатах', 'контролирование процесса').

В России, когда Джек примет участие в создании совместного предприятия, он будет рассматривать ситуацию как ситуацию изменяющуюся и предполагающую изменения. Поэтому он попытается разработать совместно со своими русскими партнерами концепцию целей, определить вероятные зоны сопротивления и конкретные действия по достижению результатов - кто, когда и как будет действовать по воплощению идеи.

Коллеги Джека считают его специалистом в деловом общении - он умеет говорить и слушать конструктивно. Для развития этих навыков Джек закончил несколько специальных курсов. И следующие несколько страниц представляют из себя его конспекты, сделанные во время обучения на этих курсах.

ЧТО ДЖЕК УСВОИЛ ИЗ КУРСА МАСТЕРСТВО ПРЕЗЕНТАЦИИ

Сегодня каждый

.... **краткость, рассеянность** внимания
.... **пассивное** мышление

Поэтому — я должен быть ДОХОДЧИВЫМ

ПРЕЗЕНТАЦИЯ ДОЛЖНА БЫТЬ КОРОТКОЙ И ПРОСТОЙ

Слова должны быть легко запоминающимися

3-Х ЧЛЕННЫЕ ОПИСАНИЯ ТИПА:	'Вера, надежда и люъовь'
АЛЛИТЕРАЦИЯ:	'Расширение рынков'
ПРОТИВОПО-СТАВЛЕНИЯ:	'Не спрашивай, что твоя страна может сделать для тебя. Спроси себя, что ты можешь сделать для своей страны!'
ПОВТОРЫ:	'Коня! Коня! Полцарства за коня!'

ПРЕИМУЩЕСТВА НАГЛЯДНОГО МАТЕРИАЛА

СЛЫШАТ ... ЗАБЫВАЮТ

ВИДЯТ ... И ПОМНЯТ

ХОД ДОКАЗАТЕЛЬСТВА

ПОЗИЦИЯ:	Согласны ли вы с моим описанием ситуации?	(Да)
ПРОБЛЕМА:	А также с моим определением проблемы?	(Да)
ВОЗМОЖНОСТИ:	Как вы видите, я исследовал все возможные пути.	(Да)
ПРЕДЛОЖЕНИЕ:	И совершенно ясно, что это наилучшее решение.	(**Да!**)

ЭТО СПЕЦИАЛЬНО ДЛЯ ВАС!

МОЯ АУДИТОРИЯ ЯВЛЯЕТСЯ САМОСФОКУСИРОВАННОЙ

ПОЭТОМУ Я ДОЛЖЕН ГОВОРИТЬ **ВЫ** КАК МОЖНО ЧАЩЕ

ВЫ, ВАШИ НУЖДЫ,

ВАШИ ИНТЕРЕСЫ ... ***ДЛЯ ВАС!***

С ВАМИ В МЫСЛЯХ...

ГЛАВНАЯ МЫСЛЬ:

ДОЛЖНА БЫТЬ КОРОТКОЙ, ДОХОДЧИВОЙ, КОНКРЕТНОЙ, ЗАПОМИНАЮЩЕЙСЯ, ВЫЗЫВАЮЩЕЙ, УВЛЕКАТЕЛЬНОЙ, ОРИГИНАЛЬНОЙ.

“Если кто-то получил незаработанный доллар, это означает что кто-то другой работал и не получил своего заработанного доллара.”

Хоффа. Из объяснений марксизма.

ВАШ ИМИДЖ И ЯЗЫК ЖЕСТОВ:

СЛЕДИТЕ ЗА ОСАНКОЙ
СМОТРИТЕ НА АУДИТОРИЮ
БУДЬТЕ УВЕРЕНЫ В СЕБЕ

ТЕХНИКА ПЕРЕГОВОРОВ — ЗАПИСКИ, СДЕЛАННЫЕ ДЖЕКОМ НА СЕМИНАРЕ

ПОДГОТОВКА К ПЕРЕГОВОРАМ

- Чего мы хотим достичь?
- Обладаем ли мы достаточной информацией о противоположной стороне и их целях?
- Что нам известно о наших конкурентах?
- Чего будут стоить нам наши предложения и что они могут дать партнерам по переговорам?
- Если мы ведем переговоры как единая команда, то как мы будем работать вместе?

ОБСУЖДЕНИЕ

- Планируя переговоры, мы используем повестку дня для изучения приоритетов наших партнеров.
- Мы наблюдаем, слушаем, задаем вопросы.
- Мы высказываем новые идеи по ходу обсуждения.
- Мы настаиваем на том, чтобы наше предложение было принято целиком - все его составные части взаимосвязаны.
- Мы не торопимся, даже если подвергаемся давлению - делаем перерывы.

ПРЕДЛОЖЕНИЯ

- Мы не начинаем до тех пор, пока у нас нет полного перечня требований партнеров по переговорам.
- Мы ставим высокие цели, чтобы результаты были адекватными.
- Мы настаиваем на своих условиях: ‘Если ..., то ...’
- На каждом этапе мы проверяем взаимопонимание - повторяем сказанное, подводим итоги.
- Никаких договоренностей по частям - соглашение не может быть достигнуто, пока нет договоренности по всем пунктам.

ПРЕОДОЛЕНИЕ РАЗНОГЛАСИЙ

- Каждая сторона должна чувствовать, что заключена хорошая сделка: все победители, нет побежденных.
- Мы тщательно определяем цену каждого предложения и контрпредложения.
- Мы твердо настаиваем на своем, но мы вежливы и дружелюбны по отношению к людям, принимающим участие в переговорах.
- Конечный результат должен быть практичным, справедливым, законным и простым в объяснении.
- Мы поступаем в соответствии с соглашением. (И мы не говорим о том, что готовы были пойти и на большие уступки.)

Джек говорит: 'Переговоры, где каждый является победителем, это замечательно, при условии что обе стороны играют по одним правилам. Если мы вместе изучаем ситуацию, то я могу найти такой вариант, который стоит мне немного, но принесет выгоду другой стороне. И мои партнеры могут сделать то же самое для меня. Все победители, нет побежденных. Но если один из нас действует по принципу 'Убей врага', ничего не получится.

ЧТО ТАКОЕ УСПЕШНЫЕ ПЕРЕГОВОРЫ — МНЕНИЕ ДЖЕКА

'Все эти собрания - дурацкая затея. Они придуманы для того, чтобы не работать и как-то убить время между чаепитиями и кофе.'

'Только взгляните на лица этих менеджеров, прибывающих на 'ежемесячные заседания по подведению итогов', и попытайтесь прочесть их мысли: 'Как бы мне отделаться без каких-либо обещаний', 'Надеюсь, они не ожидают, что я предложу им готовые идеи - в гробу я все это видел', 'В моем присутствии здесь нет никакого смысла, у меня даже не было времени прочитать повестку дня'.

‘Насколько все изменилось с тех пор, как я начал в качестве молодого стажера в бизнесе. В начале 70-х я посещал заседания, где вы бы увидели нудных бюрократов средних лет, сидящих за прямоугольными столами с карандашами наготове и ожидающих, что кто-то другой выступит с предложениями. Они воспитаны на детализированных традиционных переговорах с соблюдением множества твердых правил, и вдруг сейчас председатель призывает их чувствовать себя свободно и быть созидателями и радикалами. Жуть.’

‘Потом появились консультанты, и стол переговоров изменил форму – круглый, в виде подковы или любой другой формы, когда главное провести переговоры быстро. Это уже не конференция, а обсуждение, где председатель содействует дискуссии, а иногда и сдерживает ее, и выступает в роли арбитра. Мы же были участниками, делегатами или (Боже помоги!) представителями’.

‘Графики, белые доски, прожекторы и цветные липкие бумажки для тасовки и перетасовки и наклеивания на стенах. Мы не вели протокола, но у нас были основные пункты повестки, а также карты и личные обязательства по плану действий. Люди начали говорить о Технологичесом Процессе и Технике Решения Проблем.’

‘Это были уже стоящие, целенаправленные переговоры. И получаешь значительно больше удовольствия, чем когда слушаешь монотонный голос председателя и лицезреешь глав отделов, пинающих друг друга в спину.’

‘С сокращениями же персонала маятник качнулся немного в обратную сторону – наблюдается общее стремление к эффективности и здравому смыслу.

Изменилось и поведение людей - меньше формализма, больше открытости, чем 25 лет назад. Люди легче переходят с одного места работы на другое. (Много говорится о ‘культуре компании’, для меня же показатель такой культуры в том, каким образом проводятся переговоры.)

ПРАВИЛА ДЛЯ ЛИДЕРА ВЕДЕНИЯ ПЕРЕГОВОРОВ

- Четко определите цель, но не результат. (Если можно определить результат, то и переговоры не нужны.)
- Оповестите людей заранее, чтобы они могли подготовиться. (Убедитесь, что они знают цель переговоров и имеют необходимый материал.)
- Внимательно относитесь к выбору группы людей для участия в переговорах. (Деловые люди - для плодотворных переговоров, пунктуальные - для детализированной работы.)
- Заранее подумайте о плане, оборудовании, графике, атмосфере переговоров. (Работа лидера начинается до переговоров.)
- Начните во-время, определите твердые, но в то же время гибкие правила. (...и управляйте группой, ведите ее к цели.)

СХЕМА ОБСУЖДЕНИЯ ПРИ КОРОТКИХ ПЕРЕГОВОРАХ

(ИЛИ ОБСУЖДЕНИЕ ОДНОГО ПУНКТА ПОВЕСТКИ ДЛИТЕЛЬНЫХ ПЕРЕГОВОРОВ)

1. Свод правил; цель; все в первом стартовом блоке.
2. Фаза развития и углубления: изучение возможных вариантов, поощрение свободного мышления.
3. Подведение итогов: сокращение числа возможных вариантов, компромиссы.
4. Пути и средства: определение целей, разбор практических вопросов
5. Переход к следующей теме или пункту.

ВОВЛЕКИТЕ В ОБСУЖДЕНИЕ КАЖДОГО УЧАСТНИКА

Тот, кто говорит много, не всегда высказывает лучшие идеи. Руководитель обязан предоставить слово каждому: 'Есть еще какие-нибудь идеи? ... Кларенс, может быть у вас есть идеи? ... Правда?... Да, да... Пожалуйста продолжайте..!'

2 + 2 = 5

Если переговоры проходят успешно, каждый делится с нами своими лучшими идеями, и

МЫ ДОСТИГАЕМ РЕЗУЛЬТАТА, БОЛЬШЕГО, ЧЕМ СУММА ЕГО СОСТАВНЫХ ЧАСТЕЙ.

APPENDIX

Smirnoff

A FAMILY, A RECIPE, A BRAND AND THE VICISSITUDES OF TWO CENTURIES

Marketing in America

Smirnoff Vodka made its first impression on Western markets as the kicker in a cocktail called the 'Moscow Mule' — Smirnoff and ginger beer with a squeeze of lime served in a decorated copper mug. It was 1946, Stalin was still good old Uncle Joe, and US servicemen had come home from the war with a new taste for exotic booze.

Naturally, it was an American salesman who first concocted the product, having secured supplies of vodka, ginger beer and beakers in a series of serendipitous deals. The ginger beer and copper mug had nothing whatever to do with Moscow, but the vodka was the real thing.

ORIGINS IN MOSCOW: FROM SERFDOM TO SOCIETY IN TWO GENERATIONS

In the decade following the emancipation of the serfs in 1861, Piotr Arsenevich Smirnov, born a serf, built up his family's business — from a small distillery in a cellar at Pyatnitskaya Street, to a grander establishment by the Iron Bridge, *Chugunny Most*, the address displayed on the firm's labels. Smirnov exhibited at the 1876 Philadelphia Exhibition, and Piotr soon had permission to use the Russian state coat of arms.

At the Nizhnii Novgorod Trade Fair in 1886, Tsar Alexander III sampled the Smirnov goods and patted little Vladimir Petrovich Smirnov on the head. Smirnov's 'No 21' vodka was soon being supplied to officers' canteens, and featured at the coronation of Nikolai II and Alexandra.

Its recipe demanded painstaking filtration through charcoal, and the result was exceptionally pure.

When Piotr died in 1898, the Smirnovs were a wealthy family, employing 25,000 people and living like aristocracy.

Bolshevism, Emigration, Prohibition, Depression

After the Revolution, Vladimir was imprisoned by the Reds as an enemy of the people under sentence of death. Liberated by the Whites, he fled the country in 1918. He set up 'P A Smirnoff fils' in Poland and then Paris.

The business was sold to Rudolf Kunett, another Russian émigré, who crossed the pond to become first President of Société Pierre Smirnoff Fils of New York. He installed the first vodka plant in a former woodworking mill in Bethel, Connecticut, to coincide with the repeal of Prohibition in 1933. The first year's sales of 'white whisky' were 1200 cases — not bad in the Depression.

In 1939 the plant and the Smirnoff brand were bought for Heublein Inc. by its president John G Martin, the man who launched the Moscow Mule in 1946.

Cold War and Keeping Up with the Joneses

In 1950 there was a demonstration of New York bartenders carrying banners saying "We can do without the Moscow Mule'. Front page in the *New York Daily News*. Is there any such thing as bad publicity?

Two years later, with the Korean war over, the 'Smirnoff leaves you breathless' campaign was launched. It was the pure, easy-mixing drink to suit the era of status symbols and brunch by the pool.

Twenty years after that, Smirnoff was being sold in more than 100 countries.

Acknowledgements and Sources

Many people have lent their support and made the writing of this book a pleasant experience. First, Tanya Epissina, who saved me from many blunders, and was a sensitive translator. Dennis Malamatinas, Michael Leathes and Paul Davey at International Distillers & Vintners/The Pierre Smirnoff Company gave me their backing and let me have my head. Ann Eastman offered good advice on the penultimate draft. To all these people, thank you.

Of the numerous interviewees, I must especially thank Svetlana Ilina, Mike McLean and his team, Jan-Olov Olsson, Erik Franke, Leonardo Pavoni, Valentin Tarabara, Kyril Ivanov, Lazarus Tsiferblat, Spiros Economou, Nicholas Merica and Yevgenii Korovkin.

Quotations in the text are drawn from interviews and dozens of published sources. Particularly valuable were:

Aleksandroff, Svetlana (1993). *Business Russian*. Russian Information Services*, Montpelier

Brown, Archie, Michael Kaser and Gerald S Smith (1994) (eds). *The Cambridge Encyclopedia of Russia and the Former Soviet Union*. Cambridge University Press, 1994, Cambridge

Copetas, A Craig (1991). *Bear Hunting with the Politburo, the Real Story of Doing Business in the New Russia*. Simon & Schuster, 1991, New York

Custine, Astolphe, marquis de (1843). *Journey for Our Time*. Paris. Edited and translated by Phyllis Penn Kohler (1951). Gateway Editions, 1951, Washington

---

*Russian Information Services specialises in 'the finest Russia-focussed products and publications', and produces an excellent catalogue: *Access Russia*. RIS, 89 Main Street, Suite 2, Montpelier, VT 05602, USA. Tel: 1-800-639-430 or 1-802-223-4955. Fax: 1-802-223-6105.

Fallowell, Duncan (1994). *One Hot Summer in St. Petersburg.* Jonathan Cape, London

Glenny, Misha (1990). *The Rebirth of History — Eastern Europe in the Age of Democracy.* Penguin, London

Handelman, Stephen (1994). *Comrade Criminal, the Theft of the Second Russian Revolution.* Michael Joseph, London

Gilbert, Martin (1993). *Atlas of Russian History.* Oxford University Press, New York

Hingley, Ronald (1977). *The Russian Mind.* The Bodley Head, London

Kampfner, John (1994). *Inside Yeltsin's Russia.* Cassell, London

Kvint, Vladimir (1993). *The Barefoot Shoemaker, Capitalising on the New Russia.* Arcade, London

Noble, John and John King (1991). *USSR, a Travel Survival Kit.* Lonely Planet, Berkeley

Partos, Gabriel (1993). *The World that Came In from the Cold.* Royal Institute of International Affairs/ BBC, London

Poe, Richard (1993). *How to Profit from the Coming Russian Boom.* McGraw-Hill, New York

Remnick, David (1993). *Lenin's Tomb, the Last Days of the Soviet Empire.* Random House, New York

Richardson, Paul E (1990). *Russia Survival Guide.* Russian Information Services, Montpelier

Richmond, Yale (1992). *From NYET to DA: Understanding the Russians.* Intercultural Press, Maine

Smith, Hedrick (1991). *The New Russians.* Avon Books, New York

Thubron, Colin (1983). *Among the Russians.* Heinemann, London

Young, Cathy (1990). *Growing Up in Moscow: Memories of a Soviet Girlhood.* Robert Hale, London

THE COLOUR PLATES:

1. Universitatsbibliothek Leiden.
2. Private Collection/Bridgeman Art Library, London.
3. State Russian Museum, St Petersburg/Bridgeman.
4. Lords Gallery, London/Bridgeman.
5. Novosti Press Agency.
6. Novosti.
7. School of Slavonic Studies, London/Bridgeman.
8. Tretyakov Gallery, Moscow/Bridgeman.

We have been unable to trace the copyright holders of some of the Soviet-era images. If notified we will be pleased to amend the copyright credits in any future edition.